Better Homes and Ga

A Grower's Guide to Perennials

Text by Margaret Hanks
Photographs by Lorna Rose

MURDOCH BOOKS®
Sydney • London • Vancouver • New York

CONTENTS

KEY TO LIFE CYCLE TABLES

PLANTING: MAIN METHOD

FLOWERING

Life cycle charts are your quick guide.
For full information, consult the accompanying text.

LEFT: Brick-red rock rose grows in the front of this overflowing border, with tall yellow iris and Welsh poppies among the plants behind.

GROWING PERENNIALS

Many of the loveliest and best loved flowering plants of all are perennials. Like annuals, perennials provide a colourful display, but they have the advantage that they don't need to be changed at least twice a year. Perennials are easy-care plants and have a major place in low maintenance gardens.

Perennials remain alive for a number of years, in contrast to annuals, which usually last only one season, and biennials, which grow and flower through a second season or year. They form a variable group in terms of their size and foliage, and the flower shape, style and colour. There is a perennial to suit almost every climate, aspect and soil, and some can also be grown in containers. Perennials can be planted among shrubs, to form a background to a display of bulbs or annuals, or in separate gardens. Perennial borders are a garden staple.

ABOVE: This white form of the purple coneflower shows the unusual recurved petals.

LEFT: Bright pink marguerite daisies in the foreground and a lime green variegated lemon geranium add perennial interest to this mixed border.

PERENNIALS COMBINE here with annuals to form a brilliant border, a highlight of high summer in this lovely garden. A pink shrub rose is flanked by two varieties of Easter daisy while deep blue delphiniums add height at the back.

EVERGREEN OR HERBACEOUS?

Some perennials are evergreen but many are herbaceous. Most herbaceous perennials grow rapidly during spring and summer to flower during summer and autumn. After flowering they gradually die back to the crown or fleshy roots and remain dormant during cold winters or, in some cases, the dry season. Most of the hardy herbaceous perennials come from climates with very cold winters and so die down in autumn. In warmer areas where they do not become completely dormant and some growth continues year round, plants do not live as long. However, it is simple to renew these perennials as division is easy and most increase rapidly. A few can become invasive.

PLANTING PERENNIALS

Soil preparation

Because perennials are long-term plantings and because they are close planted, good soil preparation is essential. Although some perennials, such as astilbes and hostas, enjoy damp soil, many prefer well-drained soil. If you are planting any of the latter group, check your drainage before planting. Dig some holes in the bed, fill them with water and see how long it

PERENNIALS FOR ALL CLIMATES

COOL DISTRICTS

- Bishop's hat
- Bleeding heart
- Candelabra primula
- Cranesbill
- Globe flower
- Hosta
- Lady's mantle
- Lewisia
- Peony
- Pinks
- Solomon's seal
- Thrift

WARM DISTRICTS

- Begonia
- Bergenia
- Canna
- Daylily
- Dietes
- Gaura
- Gerbera
- Japanese windflower
- Purple coneflower
- Shasta daisy
- Stokes' aster
- Swamp rose mallow

PURE WHITE shasta daisies light up the summer garden but they also make good cut flowers for indoor decoration.

takes for the water to drain away. If there is still water in the holes twelve hours later you will need to improve the drainage by installing subsoil drains.

If the soil is very heavy clay, which remains wet but not waterlogged for a long time, you should dig in some gypsum, about 300 g per square metre. Digging in large quantities of decayed manure or compost a few weeks before planting will also improve clay soils and it is a must in sandy soils that have poor moisture and nutrient retention.

Thorough weeding of the area is essential, too, as it is difficult to remove weeds in densely planted beds. Remove the weeds you can see, dig or fork over the area again, water and wait for the next lot of weeds to emerge. You may need to repeat this step if the area has been neglected for any length of time. Hand weeding or spraying with glyphosate should eliminate most weeds, but you will need to be persistent to control oxalis, nut grass and onion weed. This sounds like a lot of work when you are eager to plant out your garden but it will be worth the wait and the effort in the long run.

Planting perennials from containers

General garden centres and nurseries will carry some perennials, especially when they are in flower. These can simply be planted out into the garden like any other container-grown plant. When the plant is removed from its pot, loosen the root ball a little so that the roots can extend into the surrounding soil. Just make sure that the planting hole is about twice the width of the container and roughly the same depth. The soil level around the plant should be the same as it was in the container. Give a thorough soaking after planting. Mulch the soil around the plant too.

Planting bare-rooted perennials

There are also nurseries that specialise in perennials. These nurseries usually have catalogues available and run mail-order businesses. They generally advertise in popular gardening magazines so that you can send for a catalogue, select your plants and place your order. Plants are available for mail order

A HIGH STONE WALL marks the boundary of this meadow garden filled with golden fern-leaf yarrow, daisies and purple loosestrife.

THESE GOLDEN-YELLOW, green-tipped spikes of a red hot poker cultivar provide a strong focus in this garden.

AN EXTREMELY TALL pink dahlia and midnight blue spires of delphinium combine with shrubs to form a backdrop for the mixture of annuals and perennials that edge this beautiful garden bed, thus demonstrating the versatility of perennials.

during their dormant season, which for the majority is from late autumn through winter. Plants are mailed, bare-rooted, packed and labelled. On arrival, they should be planted at once. If you are not quite ready to plant them, these perennials can be 'heeled in' as a temporary measure. To do this, dig a trench large enough to contain the plant roots in a sheltered part of the garden. Lay the plants on their sides in the trench, cover the roots with soil and lightly water them.

When planting bare-rooted plants again make sure the hole is at least twice the width of the root ball and deep enough to take the roots without kinking them. If some roots are very long, trim them cleanly with secateurs. Hold the plant in the hole in one hand and fill the hole, poking soil between the roots. Sometimes you can make a slight mound in the centre of the hole so that the roots can be spread out over it, keeping the crown high. Make sure the crown of the plant is not buried: if necessary lift the plant and push more soil in around the roots.

Water thoroughly immediately after planting, possibly every other day if the weather is dry and windy, but until they have developed plenty of shoot growth they will not require too much watering. The area around the plants should be mulched. If the soil has been well prepared, fertilising at this time is not necessary but you may give a very light sprinkling of blood and bone if you like.

CARE OF PERENNIALS

Perennial plantings in areas that have been well prepared need little maintenance beyond dead-heading through the flowering season to prolong blooming, and cutting back or tidying up after flowering. Established perennials do best on deep weekly watering during the growing season and fertilising in late winter or early spring as growth commences. When they become too crowded they are divided up, some time between autumn and late winter or early spring. This may be only every three or four years.

Watering

Never give perennials a light daily watering as frequent light watering will encourage surface rooting so that the plants will never develop a good, deep root system. These plants should develop big, strong root systems to carry them through several years of growth and so they benefit most from being given deep, regular watering. In very hot weather on sandy soils this may need to be twice weekly but generally once a week is ample. Mulching around the plants will also conserve moisture, as well as adding organic matter to the soil as the mulch breaks down.

Fertilising

Perennials should not need a lot of fertilising. Apply complete plant food as growth begins and if the soil has been well prepared this should be enough for the whole growing season. If your soil is very poor you may like to use a slow release granular fertiliser to feed plants slowly throughout the growing season, or to apply a second lot of complete plant food as plants start to produce flower buds. A mulch of decayed manure or compost around the plants will improve soil condition as well as supplying small amounts of nutrients to the plants. Keep the area free of weeds until the plants cover the ground. This will ensure that any fertiliser you apply is going to your perennials and not to the weeds. Avoid high nitrogen fertilisers as they tend to promote leaf growth at the expense of flowers. Rose food is ideal.

SOFT WHITE BEARD TONGUE and salvias in the foreground make a good foil for the stiff, upright growth of Russell lupins behind.

Cutting flowers and dead-heading

A number of perennials make very good cut flowers and many are grown for the cut flower trade. The various daisies, chrysanthemums, Russell lupins, delphiniums, pinks and Peruvian lilies are just a few of the perennials that are commercially grown. Regular picking of flowers does, in fact, help to ensure blooming for the longest possible time. If the flowers are not removed they will mature, most setting seed so that the flowering cycle will finish abruptly as the plant decides its reproductive work is over. If you decide not to cut the flowers but to leave them to decorate the garden, you should regularly dead-head spent flowers.

An exception to this rule are plants such as cardoon and globe thistle that have decorative seed heads. Some gardeners prefer to leave them on the plant. Many remain attractive even when dry and they can add interest to the garden in late autumn and winter.

AFTER FLOWERING

After the flowering season is over, perennials can be cut back almost to the ground.

If you are in an area prone to heavy frosts, some of the more tender perennials will then need to have the crown of the plant covered. A thick layer of straw or autumn leaves will protect it from winter damage.

In warmer areas growth continues for much longer so that plants may remain looking reasonable until early winter. Cut back hard once the weather has cooled down to allow plants some period of dormancy. Plants don't last as long in warm zones because many never become totally dormant.

THE BRIGHT, HOT COLOURS of red, orange and yellow feature in this very effective planting, which shows up so impressively against the green of the lawn. The large clump of red hot pokers and a generous drift of deep apricot-orange geum are especially notable.

INCREASING YOUR STOCK OF PERENNIALS

Division

Clumps of perennials are divided when they have become congested or when you want to take pieces for planting elsewhere. In general, most perennials need dividing about every three or four years but it can be longer. Division is done after flowering or while plants are dormant.

If you simply want some pieces to plant elsewhere you can sever a section with a knife or put a spade through the clump and lift away what you want. This way you may lose some of the peripheral pieces but the process is quick and simple. Otherwise, dig up the whole clump, shake off the excess soil and pull the clump apart or cut it into sections. Replant the sections straightaway, trimming off any very long roots. Remember that the outer growths are the youngest and in some cases the centre of the plant may have died out and can be discarded. You may need to divide very large, heavy clumps by pushing two garden forks, back to back, into the centre to prise it apart. A sharp spade may also be used but this needs a lot of force and will, of course, result in the loss of some sections of plant. This may not be of any consequence with vigorous growers.

If you are unable to replant at once or have pieces to give away, wrap them in damp newspaper or hessian and keep them in a shaded, sheltered spot, thus giving you time to decide where you want to place them. 'Heeling in', described on the previous page, is another way to store plants temporarily and they are less likely to dry out. They can, of course, be potted up in a good quality potting mix.

Taking cuttings

Many perennial plants can be grown from cuttings and a number of them, including geraniums and marguerite daisies, are among the easiest of all plants to strike. Begonias, many salvias, gazanias, pinks and chrysanthemums are others that will grow readily from cuttings.

Make up a mix of two or three parts of coarse washed river sand and one part of peat or coconut fibre peat. Put the prepared mix into clean pots, preferably no larger than 10 cm across. A pot of this size will take a number of cuttings and there will not be an excess of mix to remain too wet.

Take tip cuttings of unflowered shoots, no more than 5 to 10 cm long. Cut, don't tear, pieces from the parent plant. Take the cuttings early in the morning, dropping the pieces into a clean plastic bag, and then get them into a cool, shaded place as soon as possible. Trim the cuttings by removing the lower leaves and allowing just a very few to remain on top. Cleanly cut the base of the cutting below a node (leaf junction). Another aid to rooting is to 'wound' the cutting by carefully scraping about 1 cm of the outer bark or stem cover low down on the stem. Hormone rooting powders can be used but are not usually necessary with many of these plants.

Use a clean stick or pencil to make a hole in the mix for the cutting. Put the cutting in the hole and carefully firm the mix around it. Once you have all your cuttings in the pot you can water it thoroughly and put the pot in a warm, sheltered place out of direct sun. In the warmer months plants such as geraniums and daisies may be well rooted after three weeks, but many plants can take a considerable time to root. Check regularly each day to see if the cuttings need water but don't keep them wet or they will rot.

DIVIDING A CLUMP

Step 1: *Use a garden fork to lift the whole perennial clump from the garden bed.*

Step 2: *Separate matted clumps by inserting two garden forks, back to back, firmly into the clump.*

Step 3: *First press the fork handles together and then force them apart to split the clump in two. Repeat until the clumps are the size you want.*

Step 4: *Use secateurs to cut off dead, rotten or damaged roots. The clumps are now ready for replanting.*

STRIKING A CUTTING

Step 1: *Cut off a cutting just below a leaf node or joint. Use a sharp knife or secateurs so that the cutting is not bruised. Trim it if necessary.*

Step 2: *Make a hole in the potting mixture with your finger and insert the cutting into it. Firm the earth gently around it. If you are placing more than one cutting in the pot, space them around the edge.*

Step 3: *Water the cuttings in well but take care not to dislodge them. Make sure the water is draining away well as the cuttings will rot if the soil remains wet.*

Step 4: *To make a humid atmosphere and keep the soil and cuttings moist, make a frame of sticks or wire tall enough to cover the cuttings. Place a polythene bag over the frame and stand the pot out of direct sunlight.*

A ROMANTIC GARDEN PATH is bordered by old-fashioned favourites, including perennial daisies and pinks.

Taking root cuttings

A number of plants, including perennials such as sea lavender, matilija poppy and perennial phlox, can be grown from root cuttings. As the plant will be disturbed in taking the cuttings this is best done in winter.

- Remove soil from around the base of the plant until you come to the roots. Trace them back until they are 3–5 mm thick and cut some off cleanly with a sharp knife or secateurs. Place them in a plastic bag at once to avoid them drying out.
- Wash the soil from the roots and cut them into 3–5 cm lengths. If you intend to plant them vertically you will need to know which way is up, and so cut all the tops straight across so that you can distinguish top from bottom.
- Place the cuttings in a container vertically or lay them in horizontally and cover them with about 5 mm of propagating mix. Use the same mix as for stem cuttings. Water thoroughly and check each day to see whether further watering is needed.
- Once good shoots have appeared, your new plants can be potted up individually into small pots or planted out into the ground. It is important to keep the cuttings moist but beware of overwatering as you don't want the roots to rot.

WHAT CAN GO WRONG?

Perennials can be attacked by a number of insect pests and diseases, and problems that occur on specific plants will be discussed in the individual plant entries. Snails are one of the worst pests of herbaceous perennials as they can destroy newly emerging growth as it pushes through in late winter or spring. If each successive burst of leaves is destroyed, the plant will eventually give up. You will need to search for snails and destroy them or you can use baits if you don't have a dog.

Overwatering or poorly drained heavy soils can also damage or kill these plants, especially if they are too wet during their dormant period when there is no foliage to transpire moisture from the plant. Waterlogged soils provide ideal conditions for the growth and spread of various soil-borne root rotting fungi. A few plants, such as astilbe and canna, actually enjoy damp or boggy ground but most like to have good drainage.

Yellow leaves

- Plants may have been overwatered or they may be too dry. They may need fertilising if this has not been done for some time. Try a light application of fertiliser (in warm weather there should be an improvement within two or three weeks). If, however, the plants are suffering from overwatering, fertilising may make things worse. Towards the end of the growing season you can expect to see some leaf yellowing as they finish their useful life. Don't worry if a few leaves, especially down towards the ground, brown or yellow off during the active growth period.

Curled or distorted leaves

- Look for aphids. These are small, sap-sucking insects that may be black, brown, green or clear. They cluster thickly on the new growth of plants, sucking out the sap. This may cause curling or distortion of leaves, and flowers may fail to open if the sap has been sucked from the buds or they, too, may be distorted. Close inspection usually reveals these tiny insects and they can be squashed and wiped off the stems, hosed off or sprayed with insecticidal soap or pyrethrum based sprays. Aphids need to be controlled as they also transmit virus diseases from plant to plant.

VIOLETS never lose their appeal.

Silvery mottling on foliage

- Silvering or discolouration of foliage may be the first sign of thrip attack. These very tiny insects rasp plant tissue and suck their sap. There are several different types that cause plant damage. Apart from the physical damage caused by their feeding, some thrips are responsible for transmitting virus diseases from plant to plant. Thrip populations are greatly influenced by weather and few are active when there is heavy rain. Infestations can be severe in very dry spring weather. Many thrips use weeds as their hosts so it is important to keep your perennial beds and garden in general free from weeds. If thrips are causing damage make sure plants are not stressed through lack of water. If spraying is necessary try an insecticidal soap first then use dimethoate if necessary.

Curled and browned flowers

- Check plants for thrips as they can attack pale coloured flowers. For their control, see 'Silvery mottling on foliage'.

TAKING ROOT CUTTINGS

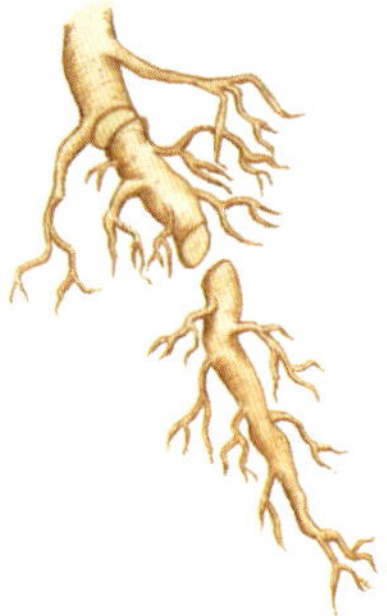

Step 1: *To take root cuttings from most perennials, trace the roots back until you can cut out a section some 3–5 mm thick.*

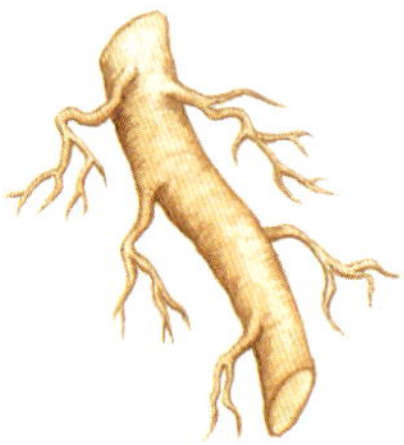

Step 2: *Wash any soil from the roots and cut them into sections 3–5 cm long. Mark the top of each so you know which way up to plant them.*

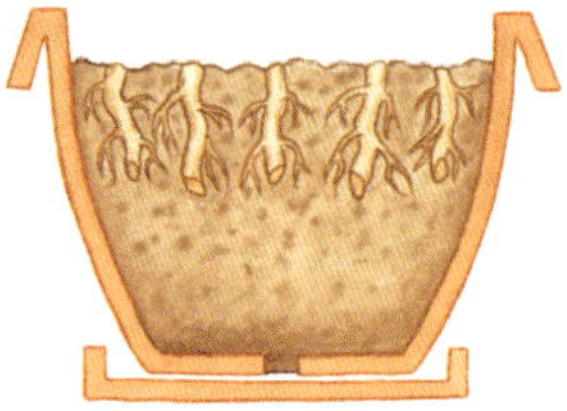

Step 3: *Place the root cuttings vertically in a container, making sure that they are the right way up. Water them in thoroughly.*

Alternatively, if plants have thin roots, take cuttings in the same way but lay them horizontally in the container and cover with a thin layer of mix.

Holes in leaves or on leaf edges

- If your plants have chewed edges or large areas of leaf missing, check them for snails. Pick the snails off and destroy them or use baits if you don't have a dog.
- If there is no sign of snails, start looking for caterpillars. Chewing insects such as caterpillars can do a great deal of damage in a short time as they can be voracious feeders. They can be well camouflaged, lying along leaf margins or hiding under leaves. Try first to find them and squash them but if damage continues try spraying with the biological insecticide *Bacillus thuringiensis* or dusting plants with derris dust before moving on to strong chemicals such as carbaryl.

Mottled leaves

- Leaf mottling may be the result of mite damage. Mites are not true insects, having eight legs like other members of the arachnid family. Mites are sap-suckers and foliage attacked by mites appears mottled and discoloured. With the aid of a magnifying glass the tiny creatures and their clear circular eggs can sometimes be seen on the underside of leaves. If severe mite attacks go unnoticed initially there may be fine webbing on the underside of foliage too. Sometimes with light attacks hosing up under the leaves every two or three days is enough to reduce their population to a non-damaging level. They are much worse in warm, dry weather or on plants that may be sheltered by the overhanging eaves of the house. Make sure that plants are well watered and well nourished. If mite numbers are out of hand you may need to spray with a registered miticide. Many general broad spectrum insecticides are useless against mites.

Grey/white powder on leaves

- This is probably caused by a common fungal disease, powdery mildew. In humid areas this disease is a constant problem. For plants that are very susceptible to this problem, much work is being done to breed resistant varieties. It may be necessary to spray with a fungicide registered for this problem or you can dust plants with sulphur (but only if the temperature is not above 28°C). If you have a problem with powdery mildew, avoid watering plants late in the day so that you do not increase the humidity around them overnight.

MARGUERITE DAISIES are prolific.

Black or dark spots on leaves

- There are many strains of fungal leaf spots that can attack a wide range of plants. If only a few leaves are affected, remove and destroy them. Avoid watering late in the day and where possible avoid watering over the foliage as the splashes of water spread the fungal spores. Many fungal leaf spots respond well to simple fungicides such as copper oxychloride but there are other effective fungicides available to the home gardener.

Yellow spots on top of leaves

- Yellow spots on the upper side of leaves that have blisters or pustules on the underside are likely to be some form of rust. There is an enormous number of rust strains and they can attack a wide range of plants and perennials, including geraniums, chrysanthemums, gerberas and pinks. It is a good idea to remove the worst affected leaves and avoid overhead watering, which splashes the spores around. Copper oxychloride will control some rusts or you may need to use a more specific fungicide.

Carroll Creek Cottage

PLANNING A PERENNIAL GARDEN

Many perennials have a long flowering period and well-planned beds of perennials can display a succession of flowers over many months. This does, however, take a good deal of planning and probably some trial and error.

If you are doing a large planting it's best to work it out on paper first so that you can place the tallest plants at the back or in the centre of a bed and so you can plan your colour scheme. You can experiment with using a variety of plants, all with flowers in one colour or shades of one colour, or you may opt for a planting of bright contrasts. Whatever you choose, allow for plenty of plants as the effect should be very full. A well-planted perennial border or garden is close planted so that every bit of soil is covered, providing foliage and floral interest throughout the season.

ABOVE: These rich purple spikes belong to the spectacular salvia 'Ostfriesland', a cultivar of Salvia nemorosa.

LEFT: Perennial daisies are repeated with lavender bushes on either side of this garden path, which is edged with thick swags of mondo grass.

IMAGINATIVE PLANNING makes the most of this garden which is shaded for a good part of the day. Tree ferns form a framework for the lush underplantings of various hostas, candelabra primulas and other shade-tolerant perennials.

USING PERENNIALS

Perennials are the most versatile of plants and the vast majority of gardeners use them in conjunction with permanent plantings of shrubs, annuals and bulbs. They are plants that require far less work and maintenance than annuals while still giving lots of seasonal colour and interest. Many low-growing perennials such as gazania, lamb's ears, pinks and bergenia make excellent border plantings while taller growers such as dietes, marguerite daisies and oyster plants can be planted among shrubs. Long-flowering plants such as gaura, kingfisher daisy, milfoil and gerbera can be planted to give colour between seasonal annual displays or to give interest to a garden bed where bulbs have finished flowering and are in the process of dying down.

PERENNIAL BORDERS

Traditionally, perennials have often been close planted in a border. To get an idea of how a well-grown perennial border should look, refer to books about the great gardens in Britain. British gardeners have been refining the art of perennial borders for a very long time and gardeners in cool climates will find plenty of inspiration there. Gardeners in warm climates will not be able to use the same plants and cannot expect the display to last as long, but they will still get ideas for both foliage and colour combinations.

FORMAL GARDENS

It is difficult for a perennial garden to look really formal but many of the best British perennial gardens have been informally planted within a formal framework. Some are enclosed within walls while many are contained within low, formally trimmed hedges. The garden beds are laid out in strict geometric style, their angular shapes defined by tightly pruned hedges, often of box or lavender. Sometimes the garden beds are defined by close-mown grass paths.

Probably the closest one can get to a formal perennial planting is with a mirror-planting effect where each part of the planting mirrors the next and the sections are divided by paths of grass, brick, gravel or stone. For a mirror planting to be successful, the whole of the area must be in full sun, otherwise there is no chance of growth rates and flowering times being the same—or as near as one can get when dealing with living plant material.

PERENNIAL GARDENS FOR WARM CLIMATES

Gardeners in warm climates cannot recreate a traditional English perennial border, as the plants available and their growth rates and ultimate sizes are so different. The flowering display of many plants is also cut short by their rapid growth and exposure to hot conditions. You will get the best results if you grow the plants you know are going to thrive rather than those that may be a poor version of the same plant in a cool area. The stronger light and greater amount of sunshine in warmer climates also mean gardens need stronger colours and bolder plantings than are usual in English borders if they are to look effective. The softer shades so popular in British gardens may look washed out.

PLANT ARRANGEMENT

Perennials come in many shapes and sizes, which is a great advantage when planning a garden. If your perennial garden is to be sited up against a fence or wall you will, of course, need to put the tallest growers at the back. For instance, delphiniums generally need to be at the back of the border. If you are making a garden in an island bed, the tall ones will need to be in the centre, with heights ranging down to the edges. Some plants such as mulleins and red hot pokers give very strong vertical accents which contrast well with lower, more variably shaped plants. Striking foliage plants such as cardoon and honey flower are grown more for their strong structural shape than for their flowers. These are big plants that must be sited carefully and probably not used to excess. A contrast in leaf colour, shape and texture will also add interest to the perennial garden. If you have the luxury of being able to create a very large or long perennial border you will need to think about repeating some of the shapes and colours to tie it all in together.

Everyone would love to have a garden that was in flower for months at a time. Planning to ensure a succession of blooms over many months is the hard part of designing the garden. Even if you consult books, a reliable local nursery and experienced gardeners, plants behave differently in different situations so that in the end it is personal experience that counts. Prior research will provide some guidance and it is worth taking a walk around your neighbourhood to see what other people are growing successfully. However, the great thing about perennials is that you can move them around when they are dormant, or in less active growth, if you are not satisfied with their appearance or performance.

USING COLOUR

Colour is, of course, a most important consideration. If you are making a large perennial garden it is a good idea to put your planting suggestions on paper, even using coloured pencils or paints to help you see how the colours work in together. You don't need to be an artist as rough shapes or blobs of colour will do. You would not want or expect to have all the plants in flower at the one time but you need to think about overlapping flowering times when considering colour.

If you want a cool looking garden you could restrict yourself to white, blue, cream or pale pink flowers, with some silver foliaged plants as accents. Red, yellow and orange flowering plants will give you a hot and vibrant look. Sometimes the addition of an area of very strong colour lifts the garden out of the ordinary, and colours in nature rarely clash. Some very famous long perennial borders cover a wide colour range starting with very soft pastel colours and ending with strong, hot colours. Another idea is to position clumps of the same plant at intervals along a border as the repetition adds to the effect of the design. Even if you have only a small space to work with, you will find the repetition gives more form to the garden.

BLUE LUPINS and white poppies here provide cool contrast with the bright reds and yellows in the extensive plantings behind.

PERENNIALS FOR ALL SEASONS

At every season of the year there is some perennial plant in flower. Winter brings the delicate and subtle beauty of the winter or Lenten rose (*Helleborus* spp.) and also bergenia in mild areas. Spring brings a succession of flowers in both warm and cool districts. Columbines, thrift, Solomon's seal, candelabra primula, geum, pinks and coral bells are just a few of the lovely spring-flowering perennials. Summer brings bergamot, milfoil, balloon flower, canna and gerbera, some of which flower well into autumn. Autumn perennials include chrysanthemums, favoured for their garden display and for picking, while red hot pokers, stonecrop and Easter daisy provide colour and interest at a time when annuals are either being pulled out or planted for the next season. These autumn-flowering perennials, along with some autumn-flowering bulbs such as belladonna lilies and nerines, will carry your garden beautifully into winter.

Perennials generally combine very well with bulbs, as bulbs that flower in late winter and spring provide foliage and blooms while perennials that flower in spring and summer are dormant or in less bushy growth. Then, when the bulb foliage is starting to go off, the perennials will be putting on growth spurts. This growth conveniently hides the less attractive dying foliage of the bulbs.

AFRICAN DAISY

Osteospermum

BRIGHT PINK African daisies have attractive and unusual deep blue centres.

AFRICAN DAISIES are the perfect plant for a nature strip. They need very little maintenance but in return give a long-lasting and prolific floral display.

FEATURES

Known as veldt daisy in its native South Africa, this is one of the toughest and most easy care of all perennials. Often used as a groundcover, it is also ideal for large rockeries, the front of borders or for growing on street fronts or steep embankments. Although capable of growing up to about 80 cm high, it is usually around 30 cm high and spreads to at least 50 cm wide, usually more. The most commonly grown species, *O. ecklonis*, produces blue-centred white daisy flowers streaked blue on the underside. *O. barberae* has cerise purple flowers, also with deep blue centres. There are a number of cultivars available with flowers in various shades of pink, including the novelty, 'Whirligig' with its quilled petals forming a wheel shape.

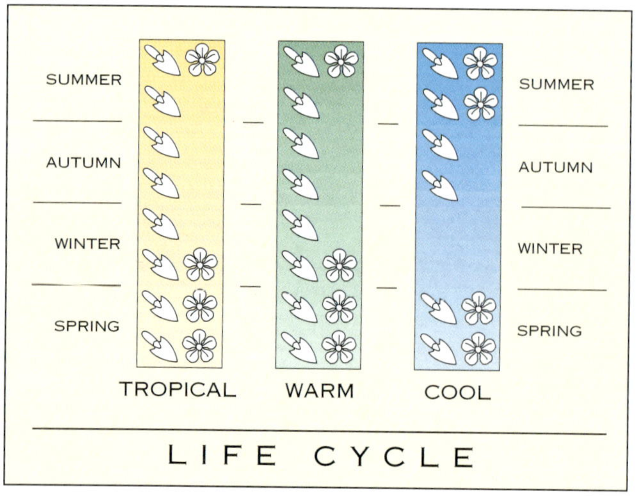

CONDITIONS

Climate Grows in tropical and warm zones and on sheltered sites in cool zones. Where frosts are severe, strike some cuttings before winter and keep them under protection.

Aspect Prefers full sun all day. Tolerates exposed windy areas.

Soil Is not fussy about soil but the soil must be very well drained.

GROWING METHOD

Propagation Grows easily from firm tip cuttings taken almost any time of year except midwinter. In cool zones cuttings should be made not later than early autumn.

Watering Water regularly to establish and then water only in long spells of hot, dry weather.

Fertilising Probably grows best without supplementary fertiliser but if the soil is extremely poor, apply a little complete plant food in spring.

Problems No specific problems are known.

FLOWERING

Season There is a long flowering period from late winter through until early summer, with odd flowers being produced at other times.

Cutting Flowers are unsuitable for cutting.

AFTER FLOWERING

Requirements After the main flowering give plants an overall clipping or shearing to maintain compact growth. Cut back rampant growth at any time.

AGAPANTHUS

Agapanthus orientalis

THE BLUE AND WHITE flowering heads of agapanthus are each composed of numerous individual flowers.

THIS DENSE PLANTING of agapanthus needs little attention and yet rewards the gardener with its wonderful summer flowers.

FEATURES

Evergreen agapanthus has dark green, strap-shaped leaves that grow to about 50 cm long. It produces rounded heads of blue or white flowers atop stems 1 m or more high, but even without the flowers it makes a great foliage accent in the garden. It is one of the toughest plants known, thriving even under very poor conditions. Agapanthus can be used to stabilise soil on steep banks, to line a drive or it can be planted in large drifts. It can also be grown in containers. A number of attractive dwarf forms have foliage rarely taller than 20 cm. These, of course, make excellent border plants.

CONDITIONS

Climate Prefers a warm to hot climate but also grows in temperate regions.

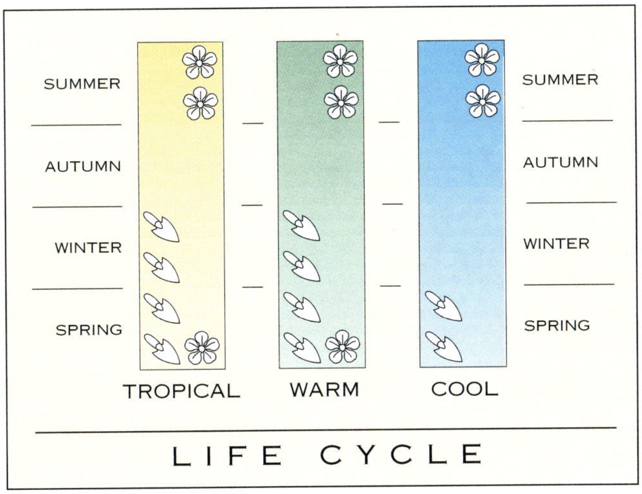

Aspect Grows in sun or shade but flowering will be poor in heavy shade.

Soil Grows in almost any soil but well-drained soil with added organic matter would be ideal.

GROWING METHOD

Propagation Divide clumps in late winter or early spring, ensuring that each division has a crown and some roots. Roots can be shortened and some outer leaves removed if necessary. Plant about 25 cm apart. Also grows from ripe seed sown in autumn or held over until spring.

Watering Needs regular water to establish but once established copes with long, dry periods. However, for the best growth and blooming give deep, weekly watering.

Fertilising Apply complete plant food in late winter or early spring if you like. Potted plants may be better with slow release granules or liquid fertiliser monthly.

Problems There are no particular problems but clumps will harbour snails.

FLOWERING

Season Blooms appear between late spring and middle to late summer, depending on the climate.

Cutting Agapanthus can be used as a cut flower if stems are plunged into boiling water for 15 seconds after cutting. They are often in full bloom at Christmas and are a feature of decoration for this season.

AFTER FLOWERING

Requirements No pruning needed other than cutting off spent flower stems and dead leaves.

ASTILBE

Astilbe hybrids

SOFT AND FEATHERY, the pale pink plumes on this astilbe will provide a long display when grown in cool climate gardens.

UPRIGHT SIDE BRANCHES are an unusual feature of this deep pink astilbe cultivar. They give the plant a rather stiff appearance.

FEATURES

This herbaceous perennial revels in moist soil and light shade although it can be grown in an open, sunny position in a cool climate as long as it is not short of water. The shiny, compound leaves are attractive in themselves, but astilbe also bears tall plumes of soft flowers 50 cm or more in height, in shades of pink, red, mauve and white. They look best when mass planted and are ideal for surrounding ponds or for naturalising under trees. They can be used as cut flowers but are probably best left in the garden where their decorative effect can be enjoyed for much longer. Not all varieties perform well in warmer districts but the deep crimson cultivar 'Granat' seems to do remarkably well.

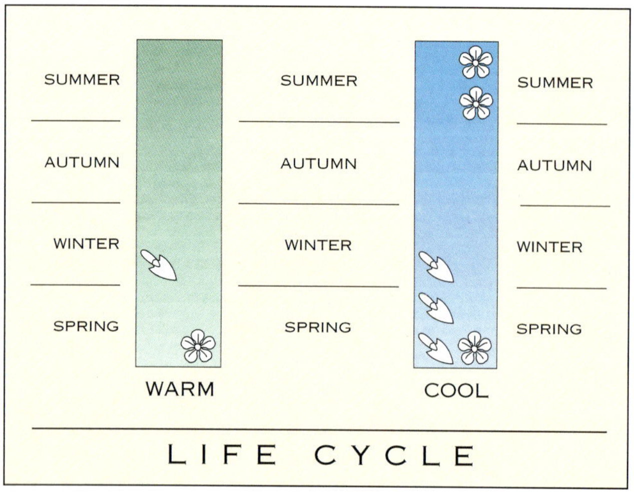

CONDITIONS

Climate Prefers cool, moist climates but is worth trying in warm areas.

Aspect In cool to cold zones grows in the open but in warmer areas must have shade.

Soil The ideal soil is rich in organic matter and retains plenty of moisture. Mulching is essential for these plants.

GROWING METHOD

Propagation Divide clumps in late winter, ensuring that each division has a crown and some roots. Plant at 20–25 cm spacings.

Watering Needs plenty of water throughout spring and summer or it will die out.

Fertilising Apply blood and bone as growth starts in spring and repeat six to eight weeks later.

Problems No specific problems are known.

FLOWERING

Season Flowers from late spring through summer. Flowers last well in summer in cool climates.

Cutting Flowers can be cut for indoor decoration.

AFTER FLOWERING

Requirements Cut out spent flower stems at ground level. As foliage dies down, it too can be cut down to the ground. Place a thick mulch of rotted compost or manure over the crown. In cold climates this provides frost protection, in warmer areas it will improve soil conditions.

Balloon Flower

Platycodon grandiflorus

MANY FORMS of balloon flower are available, but the simple, open bells of this blue one are very appealing.

THIS WELL-ESTABLISHED CLUMP of balloon flower is supported by stakes so as to show its flowers to best advantage.

FEATURES

Also known as Chinese bellflower, this herbaceous perennial grows around 50–60 cm high but much taller in perfect conditions. A more compact dwarf form growing to about 30 cm is sometimes available. Balloon flower has a long flowering period throughout the summer and the open bell-shaped flowers come in a range of blue shades but also in white and pale pink. Flowers last well when cut. There are many named cultivars available, including some double and semi-double forms. This is a lovely plant for the summer border or for planting in groups among shrubs or annuals. Clumps are compact and spread slowly, and so they are best planted where they can remain undisturbed for some years.

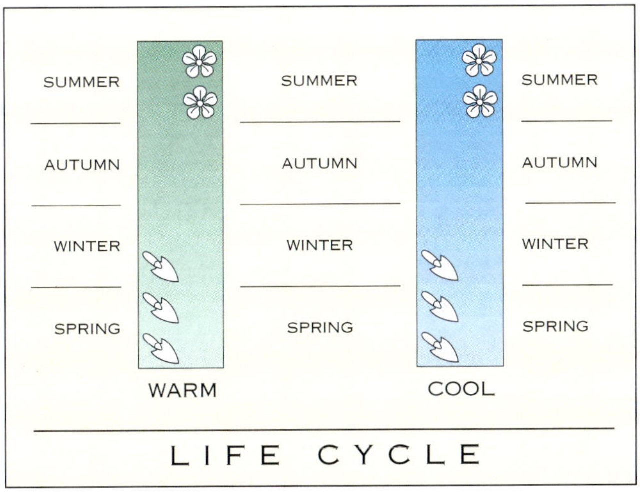

CONDITIONS

Climate Prefers a cool to cold climate but can be grown in some warmer regions.

Aspect Grows in sun or dappled sunlight. It needs protection from sun at the hottest time of day.

Soil Grows best in a well-drained soil enriched with plenty of organic matter.

GROWING METHOD

Propagation Grows from seed sown in spring and from cuttings of new growth emerging in spring. Doubles must be grown from cuttings. Clumps can be lifted and divided in late winter. Replant the divisions about 20–25 cm apart.

Watering Give regular watering during dry spring and summer weather but never allow the ground to become waterlogged.

Fertilising Apply complete plant food when growth starts in spring.

Problems No specific problems are known.

FLOWERING

Season There is a long flowering lasting from early to late summer.

Cutting Flowers can be cut for the vase.

AFTER FLOWERING

Requirements Cut back spent flower stems and then the whole plant to the ground as growth dies off. In very cold areas mulch the remaining crown with straw or coarse compost for protection.

Beard Tongue

Penstemon species and hybrids

MANY MONTHS of bloom can be expected from this fine red beard tongue cultivar if it is cut back after the first flowers have faded.

A GENEROUS PLANTING of the cultivar 'Swan Lake' makes a perfect surround for this small ornamental fountain.

FEATURES

This very large group of perennials consists of 250 species and countless cultivars, all originating in a wide variety of habitats in the southern and western United States. Their tubular or funnel-shaped flowers come in a range of shades of pink, red, purple, lavender, blue and white, some with a contrasting throat. Nowadays there is a large range of lovely cultivars in many of these shades although they may not be available in your local nursery. Beard tongues have a long flowering period through summer, especially if the spent blooms are regularly removed, but many plants can be short-lived. Beard tongues can be used in massed borders or planted among shrubs or annuals. The various species and hybrids may grow anywhere from 10 cm to 1 m high.

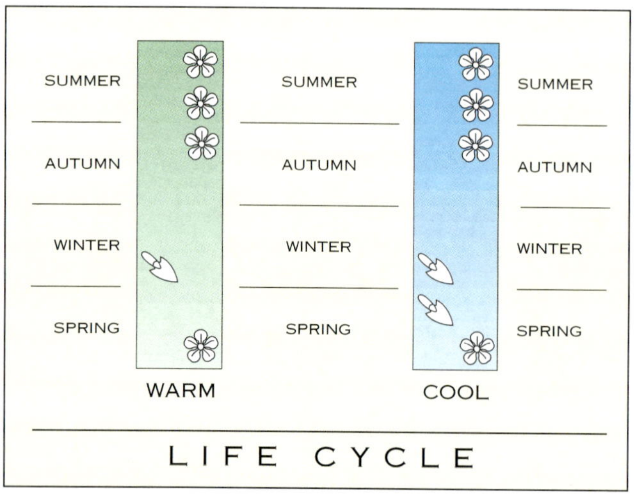

CONDITIONS

Climate Not suitable for the tropics but can be grown in warm to cool zones.

Aspect Grows best in full sun with protection from strong wind. Plants do not thrive in shade.

Soil Needs very open and well-drained soil.

GROWING METHOD

Propagation Divide plants in late winter and space them 15–30 cm apart. Some species grow well from cuttings. Seed, which is sown in late summer or autumn, is sometimes available too.

Watering Water regularly until plants are established, then it is better to water heavily every week or two rather than sprinkle often. Requirements vary with species but all will die of root rots if overwatered or if the soil is very heavy.

Fertilising Apply blood and bone or complete plant food as growth commences in spring.

Problems No specific pest or disease problems are known but root rots are reasonably common.

FLOWERING

Season Most have a fairly long flowering period from late spring through summer; for most types regular dead-heading prolongs it into autumn.

Cutting This is not a satisfactory cut flower.

AFTER FLOWERING

Requirements In autumn remove dead stems at ground level. In frosty zones growth may be burnt off; in warm areas cut it back either in autumn or in late winter.

BEGONIA
Begonia

THE DELICATE pale pink and white flowers on this pretty Begonia x fuchsiofoliosa *will be carried all through spring and summer.*

THE REDDISH STEMS and dark crimson undersides to the leaves make Begonia scharfii *attractive even out of flower.*

FEATURES

Of the thousand species and thousands of cultivars of begonia there is a large group that grows from rhizomes, a thick type of root that scrambles over the soil surface. This group includes the Rex begonias and the Iron Cross begonia, *B. masoniana*, that have beautifully patterned leaves. Most of this group can only be grown outdoors in the tropics and in sheltered microclimates of warm zone gardens. Other begonias that grow from fibrous roots but also produce small rhizomes are the perennial subshrubs, including *B. scharfii* and *B. fuchsiofoliosa*. To get an idea of the huge range of begonias available you will need to go to a begonia show or contact a specialist society. Begonias are ideal for shaded, sheltered borders or for growing among other shrubs and trees. Once established, they are very trouble-free. Most begonias have flowers that are white or in shades of pink and red. Plants range in height from a few centimetres to 1 m or so.

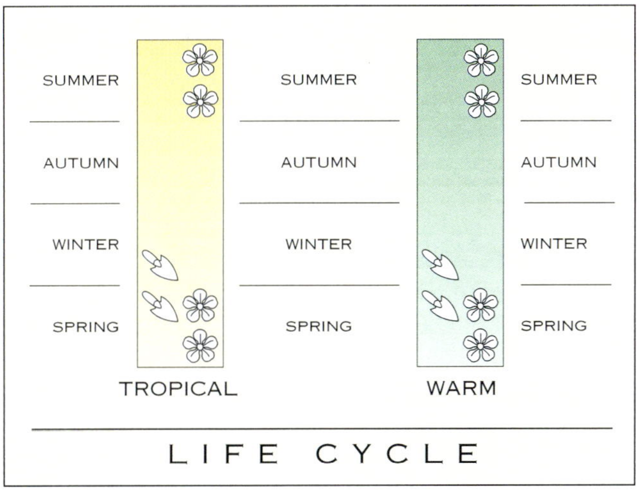

CONDITIONS

Climate Strictly a glasshouse plant in cool climates but grows outdoors in the tropics and in warm, sheltered sites in warm zones.

Aspect Needs filtered sunlight or light shade, with shelter from wind.

Soil Must have free-draining soil that contains plenty of decomposed organic matter.

GROWING METHOD

Propagation Lift and cut sections of the thick, fleshy rhizome, with some fibrous roots attached, in late winter or early spring. Whole sections of plant can also be lifted, divided and replanted 10–40 cm apart, according to ultimate size. Firm-tip cuttings can be taken of many species at any time of year although they may be hard to strike in winter.

Watering Keep soil just moist through the warmer months but it must never be waterlogged.

Fertilising Apply a little blood and bone or slow release granular fertiliser in early spring.

Problems Overwatering will cause plants to rot. Sometimes powdery mildew may be a problem. If this occurs improve air circulation, avoid watering late in the day and use a registered fungicide if necessary.

FLOWERING

Season These plants produce fine sprays of flowers in spring or summer but these begonias are grown for their foliage, not their flowers.

Cutting Flowers are unsuitable for cutting.

AFTER FLOWERING

Requirements Trim off spent flower heads and dead leaves.

Bergamot

Monarda didyma

THE HOT-PINK FLOWERS on this bergamot are easy to place in the garden. They'll combine well with other pinks, blue or white.

FOR COLOUR over a long period, this brilliant red variety of bergamot, 'Cambridge Scarlet', is hard to beat. It requires little care.

FEATURES

This is an aromatic herbaceous perennial which is also known as bee balm and Oswego tea. The name bee balm refers to its nectar-rich flowers, which are very attractive to bees, and Oswego tea to its use by the Oswego Indians and early colonists of North America as a tea substitute. Growing from 60 cm to over 1 m high, bergamot has a long flowering period through summer. The heads of tubular flowers are red, pink, white or purple with some outstanding named cultivars, including 'Cambridge Scarlet' and 'Croftway Pink'. It is easy to grow. Being a member of the mint family its roots spread vigorously but it is a great addition to a mixed planting for its long floral display. Despite its name, oil of bergamot comes from a species of citrus, not from this plant.

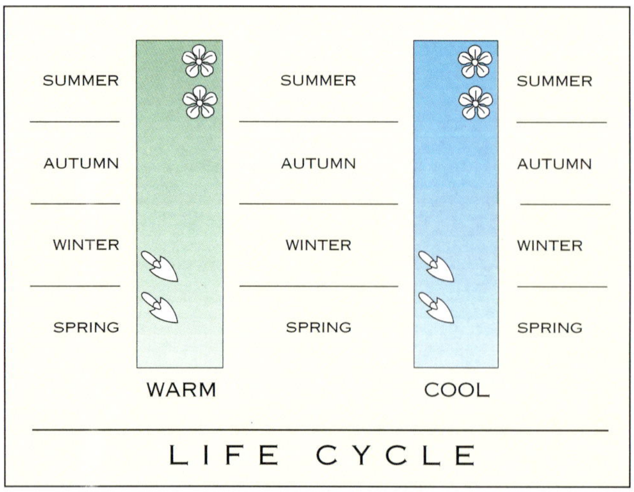

CONDITIONS

Climate Prefers a cool, moist climate but grows well in warmer areas.

Aspect Grows in either full sun or semi-shade but flowering will be best in the open.

Soil Needs well-drained soil that is made moisture retentive by the addition of large amounts of decayed organic matter.

GROWING METHOD

Propagation Lift and divide clumps in late winter or early spring. Replant the young, outer growths 20–30 cm apart. Plants usually need dividing every two or three years. Bergamot may be grown from seed sown in autumn or early spring but this does not come true to type.

Watering Needs regular, deep watering through spring and summer.

Fertilising If the soil is well supplied with humus, little fertiliser is needed. Apply some complete plant food in spring when new growth commences.

Problems Snails love to eat the new growth as it appears so take precautions. Mildew can be a problem at times. Keep the area free of dead or diseased leaves. You may need to use a fungicide spray.

FLOWERING

Season Has a long flowering period through summer.

Cutting Flowers do not cut well.

AFTER FLOWERING

Requirements Prune off spent flower stems. Cut plants back to ground level once growth begins to die off.

BERGENIA

Bergenia species and cultivars

THE WELL-DEFINED, SOLID SHAPE of bergenias makes them ideal edging plants, as this neat row beside a path demonstrates. Bergenias have other advantages, too, in that they flower in the shade and from midwinter on, both features that are not common among perennials.

FEATURES

This evergreen perennial is an asset to any garden because it flowers from midwinter into spring. The large, oval or heart-shaped leaves grow from thick stems (rhizomes) which root down as they grow. The long-lasting flowering stems grow from 30 to 45 cm tall. The main varieties grown are *B. cordifolia*, *B. purpurascens* and *B.* x *schmidtii*. All have flowers in shades of pink or mauve-pink, although there are some lovely cultivars with rosy pink to red blooms. Bergenia is an ideal plant for bordering garden beds or for growing in large clumps in a shady rockery. This is a very easy-care plant and one that is long lived. Some people call these plants elephant's ears but that common name more properly belongs to the very large aroids *Colocasia* and *Alocasia*.

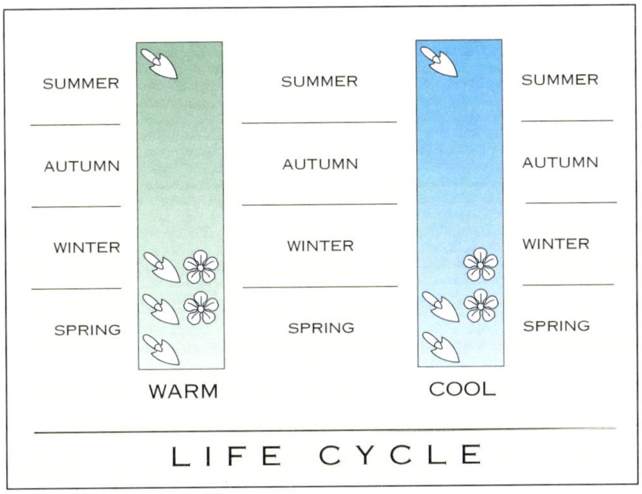

CONDITIONS

Climate Grows best in cool to warm zones. It is not suited to the tropics or the subtropics.

Aspect Prefers shade or semi-shade as the somewhat fleshy leaves burn in hot sun.

Soil Needs soil that is well drained and preferably enriched with organic matter.

GROWING METHOD

Propagation Grows from divisions of an existing clump or from cuttings of a stem with a leaf attached in spring after flowering is finished. With either method, cut away half the leaf to reduce moisture loss unless your piece has a very small leaf. Space plants 15–20 cm apart.

Watering Needs regular, deep watering during dry spring and summer weather.

Fertilising Apply complete plant food or blood and bone in spring.

Problems Snails can be a problem in damp weather. Search for snails in the plant clumps or use snail baits if you do not have a dog.

FLOWERING

Season The long lasting flowers appear from midwinter to spring.

Cutting A good cut flower but flowers will last longer and give better decorative value in the garden.

AFTER FLOWERING

Requirements No pruning is needed beyond removal of the spent flower stems.

BISHOP'S HAT
Epimedium

NEW GROWTH on bishop's hat plants bears attractive bronze or pink shadings but the older foliage is plain green.

A DENSE CARPET of bishop's hat makes a wonderful groundcover under this grove of small trees.

FEATURES

This low-growing perennial is grown more for its attractive foliage than its flowers, although the flowers are very dainty. The flower shape resembles a bishop's mitre, giving rise to the common name. Many species have small, starry flowers in white, cream or yellow although there are pale and rose-pink varieties too. This is a woodland plant and it makes a good groundcover or filler for shaded parts of the garden. Some die down completely in winter while others remain evergreen. Plants are rarely more than 30 cm tall. Combine it with plants such as Solomon's seal, primrose or winter rose, which enjoy similar conditions. The arrow or heart-shaped leaves may have bronze or pinky-red colourings when young, although they become green as they mature.

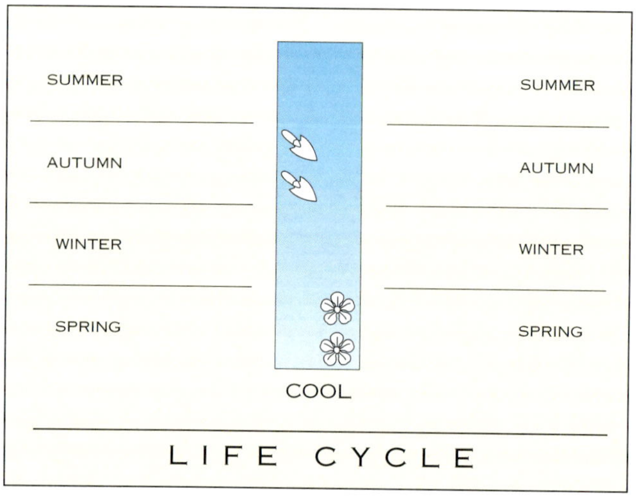

CONDITIONS

Climate This is a plant for cool, moist climates but it could be tried in a cool spot in warmer areas.

Aspect Needs dappled shade with protection from strong wind. In cold climates it may be grown in more open situations.

Soil Needs well-drained soil heavily enriched with organic matter. Regular mulching is needed.

GROWING METHOD

Propagation Clumps can be divided in autumn although with some varieties this is not easy. Pull apart or cut away sections of plant, keeping both roots and a bud or shoot on each piece. Plant 15–20 cm apart. Some species seed readily.

Watering Needs to be kept regularly watered during spring and summer.

Fertilising Apply blood and bone or slow release fertiliser as new growth begins in spring.

Problems Snails may attack soft new growth as it appears and so take precautions.

FLOWERING

Season The small flowers appear in spring along with the leaves.

Cutting Flowers can be cut for the vase and last quite well in water.

AFTER FLOWERING

Requirements Spent flower stems can be clipped off. Old, dead foliage should be tidied up at least by the end of winter.

Bleeding Heart

Dicentra spectabilis

THE ARCHING STEMS of this bleeding heart carry masses of bright pink, heart-shaped flowers shaped like tiny lockets.

THE BLEEDING HEART is well worth growing for its foliage alone as the delicate, fern-like leaves are very decorative.

FEATURES

With fern-like foliage and curving stems bearing pretty pink and white, heart-shaped flowers, bleeding heart is an all-time favourite perennial. It appeals to children and adults alike. There is a cultivar, 'Alba', which has pure white flowers. Another species less commonly grown is *D. formosa*, which has very 'ferny' foliage but its flowers are not so completely heart-shaped. Suitable only for cool climate gardens, bleeding heart can be grown in a mixed border or in the filtered shade of trees. Plants may reach 40–60 cm in height in good conditions and form a clump 50 cm or so wide. It is completely herbaceous, dying right back to the ground in autumn or early winter.

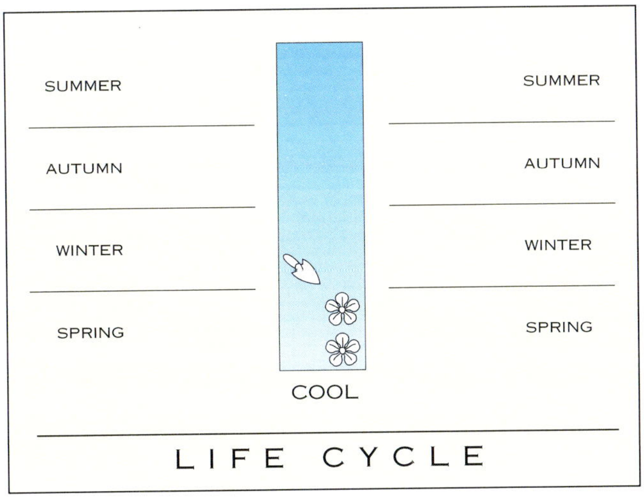

CONDITIONS

Climate Bleeding heart grows successfully only in cool to cold climates.

Aspect Grows best in filtered sunlight or morning sun and afternoon shade. Strong hot sun and strong wind make it shrivel up.

Soil Needs well-drained soil rich in organic matter. Dig in copious quantities of decayed manure or compost several weeks before planting.

GROWING METHOD

Propagation Divide large established clumps in late winter and plant divisions 25–30 cm apart. Also grows from seed sown in late summer.

Watering Needs regular, deep watering during dry periods in spring and summer.

Fertilising Apply a sprinkling of blood and bone or complete plant food whenever growth begins in spring.

Problems There are no specific pest or disease problems known for this plant.

FLOWERING

Season Blooms for several weeks during either middle or late spring.

Cutting Flowers are not suitable for cutting.

AFTER FLOWERING

Requirements Cut out spent flower stems. As foliage yellows and dies off, cut it off just above the ground.

Campion
Lychnis coronaria

THE DISTINCTIVE ARRANGEMENT of petals on Lychnis chalcedonica *has given rise to its common name, Maltese cross. The bright red flowers show up well against white or blue flowers.*

TRUE CAMPION, Lychnis coronaria, *has these cheerful, bright cerise flowers.*

FEATURES

Rosettes of soft, silver-grey foliage make campion a very useful plant in the garden and they contrast with the deep cerise or magenta flowers that appear on stems 30–40 cm high. There is also a white flowered form. Easily grown in a sunny, well-drained spot, campion tends to be short lived but it seeds itself so that you always have a fresh supply. It can be grown as a border plant or as part of a mixed perennial display where its silvery foliage makes a good contrast. This very easy-care plant establishes rapidly. *L. flos-jovis* is another species grown more for its silvery foliage than its purple-red flowers. Another popular species of *Lychnis* is the Maltese cross, *L. chalcedonica*, which has mid-green leaves and produces a rounded head of bright scarlet flowers. Pink and white forms, and a double form, 'Flore Plena', are also available.

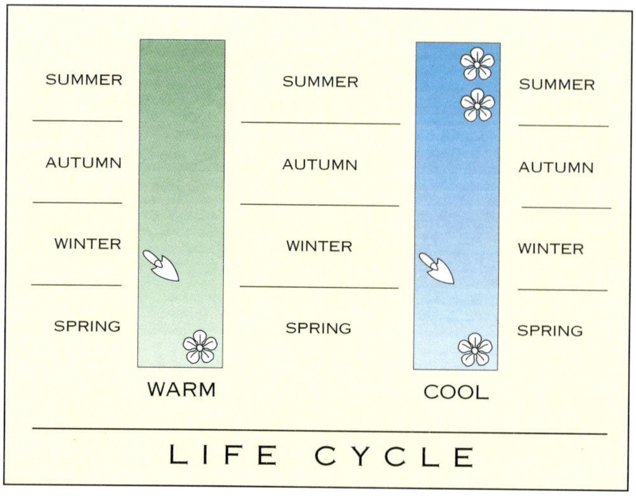

CONDITIONS

Climate Not suitable for very warm, humid districts. Grows well in cool to warm areas, and prefers areas of low humidity.

Aspect Grows best in full sun but tolerates shade for part of the day.

Soil Needs very well-drained soil, but the soil need not be rich.

GROWING METHOD

Propagation Tends to self-seed. These plants may show variation from the parent plant. Divide clumps in late winter, discard the oldest sections and space about 20 cm apart.

Watering Needs regular watering to establish but once established needs only occasional, deep watering during very dry periods.

Fertilising Needs little fertiliser. A little complete plant food may be given in very early spring.

Problems No pest or disease problems are known but overwatering or prolonged summer rain may cause rotting.

FLOWERING

Season Flowers from late spring through summer, depending on climate. Blooming will be later and will last longer in colder areas.

Cutting Flowers are unsuitable for cutting.

AFTER FLOWERING

Requirements If you don't want plants to self-seed, dead-head constantly as flowers fade. This should also prolong blooming. Completely spent stems should be cut off as low as possible.

CANDELABRA PRIMULA

Primula

CANDELABRA PRIMULAS are happily combined here with hostas, both enjoying the damp conditions of a bog garden.

THE CHARACTERISTIC TIERS of flowers are well displayed in this good-sized planting of white perennial primulas.

FEATURES

Candelabra primulas, which produce their flowers in distinct whorls or tiers up the stems, form one group among the several hundred species of primula. Most are herbaceous, but *P. helodoxa*, which has clear yellow flowers, is evergreen. Other species in this group include *P. aurantiaca*, *P. bulleyana*, *P. japonica* and *P. pulverulenta*. Flowers may be white, or in shades of yellow, orange, pink, red and purple. Plant heights vary from 30 cm to about 1 m. These are plants that need to be placed in big groups for maximum impact. They are all at home in damp soil and are often planted around ponds or other water features. Given the right conditions these plants are not demanding and will give a great show year after year.

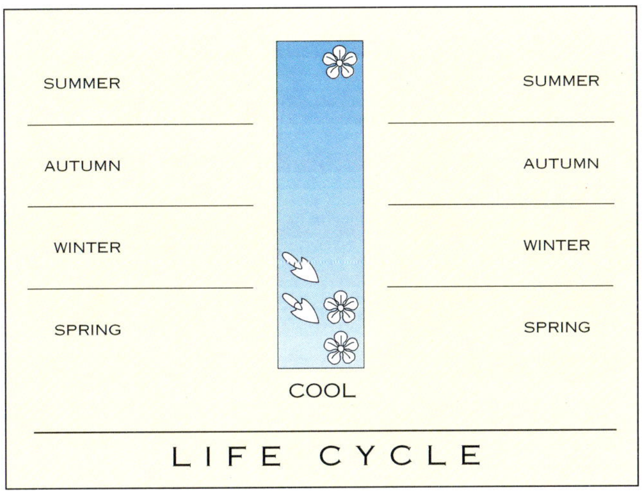

CONDITIONS

Climate This cool climate plant does not do well in warm areas.

Aspect Grows in full sun but partial shade probably suits it best.

Soil Needs deep, moisture-retentive soil that is heavily enriched with organic matter but it does not like to be waterlogged in winter.

GROWING METHOD

Propagation Lift and divide crowns in late winter or early spring and replant about 20 cm apart. Straight species can also be grown from seed sown in late summer to early autumn.

Watering Never let this plant dry out during the growing season.

Fertilising Little fertiliser is needed if soil is well enriched with humus but a little blood and bone may be given in early spring.

Problems No particular pest or disease problems are known for this plant.

FLOWERING

Season This lovely primula flowers during spring and early summer.

Cutting Flowers probably last a few days in the vase but the garden display will be more rewarding.

AFTER FLOWERING

Requirements Spent flower stems can be cut off unless you are waiting for seed to set. In good conditions many of the species will self-seed.

CANNA
Canna x generalis

THE APRICOT-ORANGE FLOWERS of these cannas will contribute a rich, flamboyant colour to the garden for many months.

THE COLOUR of these scarlet cannas is highlighted by the darker green, slightly bronzed foliage that surrounds them.

FEATURES

Formerly referred to as 'Indian shot' because of the extremely hard seed, cannas are easy to grow and provide a spectacular display of foliage and flowers over a very long period. This is a tough plant able to withstand difficult growing conditions, including waterlogged soil. Plants vary in height from 50 cm to almost 2 m. The smaller forms may be better suited to small garden spaces. The foliage, which may be burgundy, green or bronze with contrasting venation, is often used by flower arrangers and it can have greater decorative value in the garden than the flowers. The large showy flowers may be solid red, yellow, orange, pink or white, or splashed with a contrasting colour. There are also cultivars with lovely pastel colours including a soft apricot. Cannas make a great show when planted in large, bold clumps but they can also be used as highlights in a mixed border.

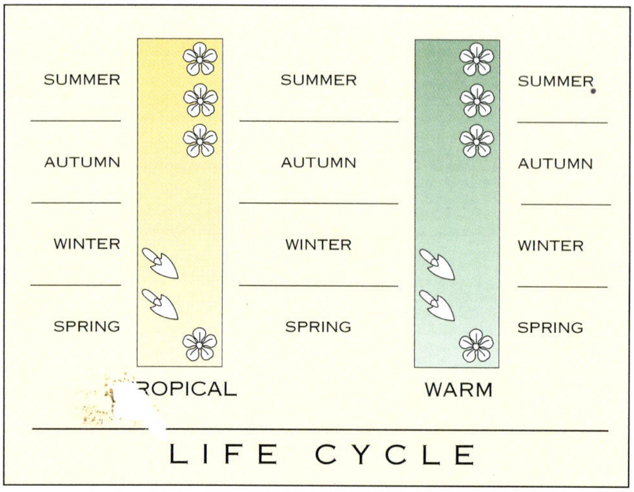

CONDITIONS

Climate Grows in almost any area from the tropics to cool regions. In cold areas lift and store the fleshy rhizome (rootstock) over winter.

Aspect Grows best in full sun all day. It also takes exposure to strong salt wind.

Soil Grows best in soil heavily enriched with organic matter. It can be planted in boggy ground to help soak up excess moisture.

GROWING METHOD

Propagation Lift and divide the rhizome into sections, each piece having a bud or eye and some roots. Plant out about 30 cm apart and 5 cm deep, preferably in late winter to early spring.

Watering Must never be short of water during the growing season.

Fertilising Apply complete plant food as growth begins in spring and mulch with decayed manure or compost. Cannas are heavy feeders.

Problems No specific pest or disease problems are known for cannas.

FLOWERING

Season The long flowering period is from late spring until early autumn.

Cutting Cut flowers don't last well but the foliage is used in large arrangements.

AFTER FLOWERING

Requirements Cut spent flower stems out at ground level. In cool areas foliage will brown and die off—cut them back to ground level, too. Although foliage may not die down in warm areas, plants will perform better if cut back hard in winter.

CARDOON

Cynara cardunculus

CARDOON LOOKS *rather like a Scotch thistle. Its purple flowers can be left to dry and then used as indoor decoration.*

THE SILVERY LEAVES *of cardoon are large and shapely, and a large clump can look almost sculptural.*

FEATURES

A close relative of the globe artichoke, cardoon is generally grown for its arching, metre-long, silver-grey foliage. Growing up to 2 m high and almost 2 m wide, it is a splendid accent plant for the back of a border or it can be combined with low-growing green plants in an open position. Both the colour and the form will stand out from other plantings. The purple, thistle-like flowers develop in summer and the dried heads left on the plant can be decorative into autumn. Cardoon is also edible, being grown for the fleshy bases of the leaves which are tied up and blanched, then eaten raw or cooked. It can be difficult to place effectively in a very small garden as it is best viewed against other plants displaying a range of different shapes, sizes and colours.

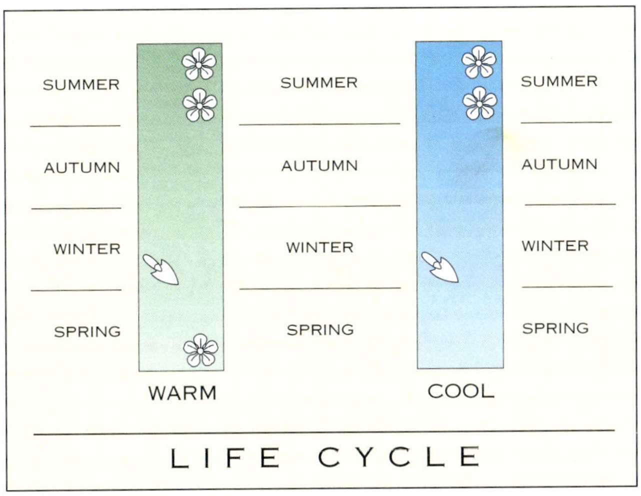

CONDITIONS

Climate Unsuitable for the tropics but can be grown in cool to warm zones.

Aspect Needs full sun all day for best results.

Soil Needs rich, well-drained soil. Before planting, dig in large amounts of manure or compost.

GROWING METHOD

Propagation Propagate in late winter by division of clumps or from suckers, or in spring from seed. Position plants at least 70 cm apart. Seed-grown plants are variable in quality and do not normally reach maturity in the first year.

Watering During the growing season regular, deep watering is essential.

Fertilising Apply complete plant food as growth commences in spring and repeat once a month. When cardoon is grown as a vegetable it is given liquid feeding weekly.

Problems No specific problems are known.

FLOWERING

Season The purple, thistle-like flowers appear during summer on stems 2–3 m high.

Cutting If flowers are allowed to dry on the plant, they can be used as indoor decoration.

AFTER FLOWERING

Requirements Once the flowers have lost their decorative value, cut off the whole stem low down. As the plant starts to die off and look tatty, cut it off just above the ground.

CARNATION

Dianthus caryophyllus

FRINGED PINK FLOWERS and silver-grey buds and stems make this a classic.

TALL GROWERS may need a light frame or thin stakes to prevent top heavy flowers lying on the ground. This frame supports several plants, thus avoiding a 'forest' of stakes in the garden.

FEATURES

Carnations are very popular both as cut flowers and as a garden subject. Flowers are carried singly or in groups on stems 30–50 cm high, although florists' carnations may be taller. Most have a lovely, clove-scented perfume, although some have little or no perfume. Flowers may be pink, red, mauve, yellow or pure white and some varieties have contrasting streaks. The foliage is a soft grey-green. Although classed as perennials, carnations become rangy and sprawling and should be repropagated every 2–3 years.

CONDITIONS

Climate Grows best in warm to cool areas with low humidity. Unsuitable for tropics or subtropics.

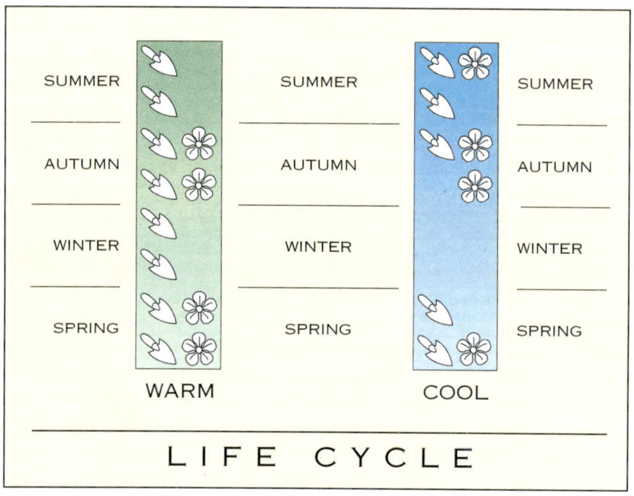

Aspect Needs full sun all day. Protect from very strong wind.

Soil Needs very well-drained soil with plenty of well-decayed organic matter. Unless soil is alkaline, apply a light dressing of lime before planting. Keep mulches well clear of stems.

GROWING METHOD

Propagation Grows easily from cuttings taken at almost any time. Use leafy side shoots and strip off all but the top leaves. Roots form in 3–5 weeks. Space newly rooted plants 20 cm apart.

Watering Water regularly to establish then occasionally in very dry weather. Carnations tolerate dry conditions well. Overhead watering encourages fungal problems.

Fertilising Little fertiliser is needed if soil contains plenty of organic matter but you may give complete plant food in early spring and midsummer.

Problems Carnation rust, a fungal disease, is common in warm humid areas. Greyish spots appear on leaves or stems and foliage may curl and yellow. Spray with a fungicide. Budworms can be a problem: squash caterpillars when seen.

FLOWERING

Season Flowers appear in spring and autumn but spasmodically at other times. Remove excess buds to produce good-sized main blooms.

Cutting An excellent cut flower. Recut stems between nodes (joints) to aid water uptake.

AFTER FLOWERING

Requirements Cut stems back to main foliage.

CHRYSANTHEMUM

Dendranthema x *morifolium*

CASCADING OVER the fence onto the erigeron below, this garden chrysanthemum gives a prolific display of flowers.

THE QUILLED PETALS are characteristic of this open 'spider' style of chrysanthemum, as is the shading of colour.

HYBRID CHRYSANTHEMUMS such as this are very popular in the cut flower trade and are available for most of the year.

FEATURES

SUMMER AUTUMN WINTER SPRING
HERBACEOUS

This chrysanthemum (*D.* x *morifolium*) probably originated in China but was introduced into Japan a very long time ago. It features widely in the art of both countries. It is the garden and florists' chrysanthemum, the feature of autumn garden displays. It is widely used as a long-lasting cut flower and is a symbol of Mothers Day in many places. Potted plants in bloom are available at most times of the year for use as indoor decoration—they are grown by specialists who manipulate growing conditions, especially the hours of light to which the plants are exposed. These chrysanthemums are 'short day plants' and will not bloom if exposed to too many hours of light. Tall varieties can grow to nearly 2 m in height but there is a great range available, including the dwarf growing 'cushion mums'.

Colours The colour range is wide, covering white, cream, yellow, many shades of pink and lilac, burgundy, pale apricot and deep mahogany. Many of the lovely singles grown for the cut flower market have pretty, lime-green centres.

Types There are many forms of chrysanthemum and they have been classified by specialist societies and nurseries according to floral type. Some of the types are decoratives, anemone centred, spider, pompom, single, exhibition and incurved Japanese.

Staking Many of the taller varieties need staking, which needs to be carefully thought out to avoid looking ugly. One method is to insert bamboo canes at intervals around and through the planting and thread twine from cane to cane in a criss-cross fashion, perhaps 50–60 cm above the ground.

CONDITIONS

Climate Grows in cool to warm districts but not in tropical areas.

Aspect Grows best in full sun with protection from strong wind.

Soil Needs well-drained soil that has been heavily enriched with organic matter before planting. Plants should also be mulched with decayed compost or manure.

THIS UNUSUAL chrysanthemum has the central petals incurved like those of the Japanese type while the outer ones are widespread.

THE RUSSET COLOURS of these flowers seem appropriate to their autumn flowering season, when the leaves are turning.

GROWING METHOD

Propagation In spring lift and divide the new suckering growth so that each new plant has its own roots and shoots. Cuttings of new growth can also be taken. Space plants 40–50 cm apart.

Watering Throughout the growing season give a good soaking once a week, or twice in lighter soils.

Fertilising Once plants are well established fertilise them every four weeks with soluble liquid fertiliser or with light dressings of complete plant food.

Problems • Small lumps on the leaves or stems may be caused by the gall midge and may develop into distorted foliage and flowers. Destroy affected plants or spray with a systemic insecticide if noticed early. Don't use the chemical dimethoate on these plants as it causes damage to the foliage.

• A number of fungal diseases can attack these plants, including leaf spot, powdery mildew, rust and white rust. Avoid overhead watering or watering late in the day and ensure that residue from previous plantings is cleared away. You may need to spray with a registered fungicide. White rust is a particularly serious disease and affected plants are probably best removed and destroyed.

• Watch for aphids clustering on new growth. Pick them off by hand, wash them off or spray them with insecticidal soap.

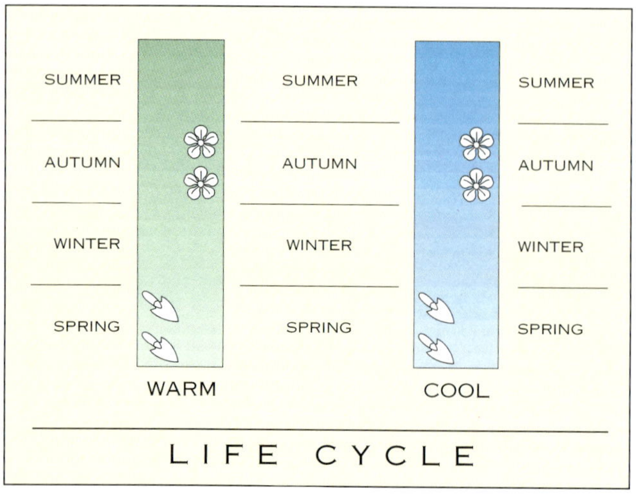

FLOWERING

Season Flowering time is middle to late autumn.

Cutting Cut flowers will last two or three weeks with frequent water changes, as long as foliage is removed from the parts of the stems that are under water. Potted plants can be bought in bloom year round and cut flowers are normally available most of the year.

AFTER FLOWERING

Requirements Once flowering has finished, cut off plants 12–15 cm above the ground and clear away all rubbish. Potted plants that have finished blooming should be cut back. They can be planted out into the garden where they should grow and flower at the normal time of autumn. If the pot plants have been indoors for some time, acclimatise them gradually by putting them where they receive only morning sun for a few days before gradually increasing the amount of exposure.

CINQUEFOIL

Potentilla

PALE SCARLET CINQUEFOIL looks quite at home here with annual heartsease, despite the different colours.

DESPITE THE SMALL FLOWERS, these bright little plants are difficult to overlook in any perennial garden.

FEATURES

There are over 500 species of cinquefoil, including annuals, perennials and small shrubs. All have the characteristic five-lobed leaf, and the single or double flowers may be white or in shades of yellow, red or pink. Cinquefoil belongs to the rose family and the foliage can be attractive even when plants are not in flower. They may be from 5 to 50 cm or more high. The short types make good edging plants while the taller ones can be used successfully in a mixed planting. Flower stems tend to flop over and so may need light support: wire hoops or twine tied around three light canes are a good choice. Many red cinquefoils are hybrids of *P. atrosanguinea* while some yellows derive from *P. argyrophylla* and *P. recta*. Some cinquefoils tend to self-seed but unwanted plants are easily removed.

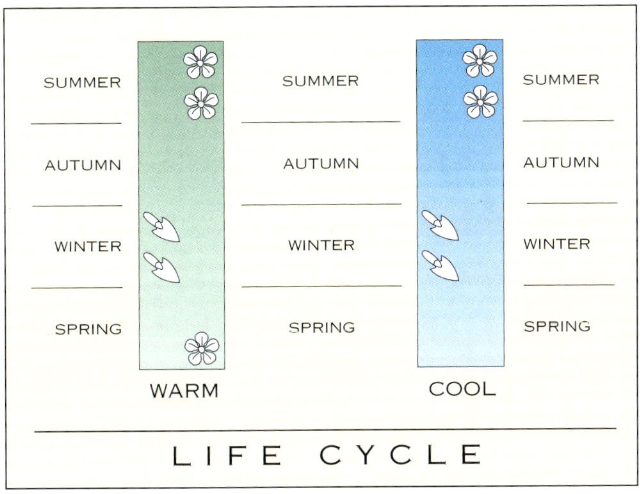

CONDITIONS

Climate Suitable for cool to warm regions only.

Aspect Needs full sun in cool regions but tolerates some shade in warmer districts.

Soil Needs well-drained soil enriched with some organic matter.

GROWING METHOD

Propagation Species and single-flowered varieties grow from seed or runners. Sow seed or remove runners in late summer or early autumn. Hybrid doubles must be grown from divisions made during middle to late winter. Plant spacing depends on ultimate size and may be anywhere from 15 to 40 cm.

Watering Needs regular, deep watering in dry weather during spring and summer but soil should never remain wet for long periods.

Fertilising Apply complete plant food as growth commences in spring.

Problems No particular problems are known.

FLOWERING

Season Flowers may begin in late spring in warm districts, but the main blooming time is during summer.

Cutting Flowers do not last well when cut.

AFTER FLOWERING

Requirements Cut off spent flower stems at ground level and tidy up plants as the growth begins to die off. In milder areas the foliage may not die off completely.

COLUMBINE
Aquilegia x hybrida

WIDELY CONTRASTING COLOURS are combined in the dainty flowers of this modern long-spurred hybrid columbine.

WOODLAND PLANTS, columbines are here in an ideal setting that allows both flowers and foliage to show to advantage.

FEATURES

These old-fashioned favourites, also known as granny's bonnets, give a lovely display in the garden and make very decorative cut flowers. The pretty foliage is grey-green and the flowers come in a range of single colours—white, pink, crimson, yellow and blue—and combinations of pastel and brighter shades. The older forms have short-spurred flowers that resemble old-fashioned bonnets, especially the quaint 'Nora Barlow', a double which is a curious mix of red, pink and green. Modern hybrids are long spurred and are available in many single colours and bicolours. Plants may be 40–70 cm high. Columbines are not long lived but are easily raised from seed. They are ideal for the shady garden and can be planted in clumps under deciduous trees or in mixed borders. Although herbaceous perennials, they are treated as annuals in some warm areas.

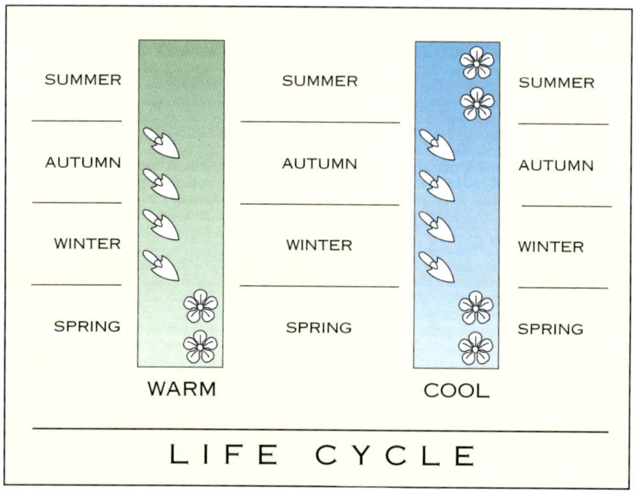

CONDITIONS

Climate Grows best in a cool, moist area but also does well in warm regions. Unsuitable for the tropics or arid inland regions.

Aspect Prefers semi-shade but will take full sun in cool areas or mountain districts.

Soil Needs well-drained soil that contains plenty of organic matter.

GROWING METHOD

Propagation Clumps are hard to divide but this can be done in autumn or late winter. Grows also from seed sown in autumn. Self-sown plants are hardy but may not be true to type. Space plants about 30 cm apart.

Watering Needs an ample supply of water in dry weather through spring and summer.

Fertilising Apply complete plant food in spring as new growth begins.

Problems No particular pest or disease problems are known for this plant.

FLOWERING

Season There is a long flowering period from mid-spring to midsummer.

Cutting Flower stems can be cut for the vase but the garden display is longer lasting.

AFTER FLOWERING

Requirements Spent flower stems can be removed or left on the plants for seeds to mature but be warned that plants can produce a prodigious number of seedlings. Cut back old growth to ground level as it dies off.

Coral Bells

Heuchera sanguinea

DAINTY LITTLE PINK FLOWERS are massed above the attractive foliage to make coral bells an excellent choice for the front of a border or garden bed. Here they are planted to provide a foil for the abundant blooms of white roses behind.

FEATURES

This perennial forms a low rosette of lobed leaves which make a neat plant suitable for edging or mass planting at the front of the border. The foliage is evergreen and the plants are reasonably long lived. Established mass plantings produce a striking display of blooms over quite a long period. The flower stems, which stand high above the foliage, may be from 30 to 45 cm high. The species has red flowers but there are cultivars available with pink, white or deeper crimson blooms. Other species of *Heuchera* are used in breeding some of the cultivars. All the plants in this group are native to the United States, most to the northwestern area.

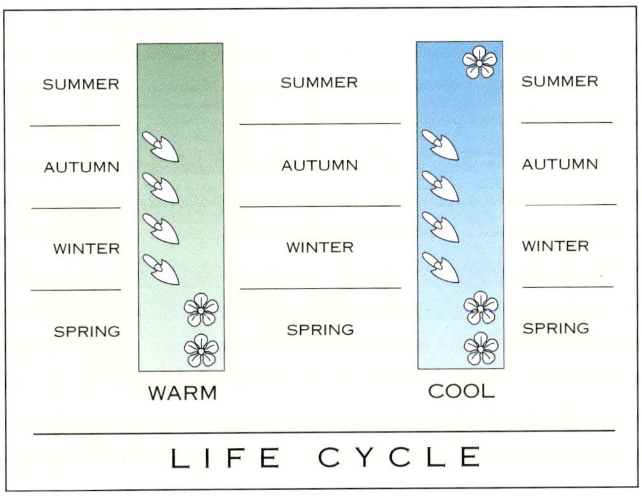

CONDITIONS

Climate Grows best in a cool climate but is worth trying in warm areas.

Aspect Prefers full sun but tolerates light shade. In warmer districts it will probably benefit from shade on hot afternoons.

Soil Needs very well-drained, open-textured soil. Permanently wet soil will kill this plant.

GROWING METHOD

Propagation Clumps can be divided in autumn or late winter but ensure that each division has its own roots. It can also be grown from seed sown in early autumn. Plant at 20–25 cm intervals for good effect.

Watering Needs regular, deep watering in dry weather during spring and summer.

Fertilising Apply blood and bone or complete plant food as growth commences in spring.

Problems No particular problems are known.

FLOWERING

Season It has a long flowering period throughout spring and into early summer.

Cutting Flowers do not last well as cut blooms.

AFTER FLOWERING

Requirements Remove spent flower stems once they begin to look untidy. Apart from removal of any dead leaves this is all that is necessary.

COREOPSIS

Coreopsis

COREOPSIS ARE worth considering for their appealing bright yellow flowers even though they are considered weeds in some areas.

THIS DOUBLE-FLOWERED FORM of golden coreopsis provides many weeks of bright colour through the summer.

FEATURES

Perennial coreopsis carries a profusion of bright yellow daisy flowers over a long period, mostly through summer into autumn, although some flower in spring. Regular dead-heading will ensure prolonged blooming. *C. lanceolata*, known as calliopsis, has become naturalised in many parts of the world. The strong-growing *C. grandiflora* and its double form, 'Perry's Double', may grow 60–90 cm high, *C. verticillata* about the same. There are several species worth trying, some with dwarf form or flowers displaying a dark eye. The foliage is variable, too. These plants are very easy to grow and will give a great show with little care. Plant them in bold clumps in a mixed border for best effect.

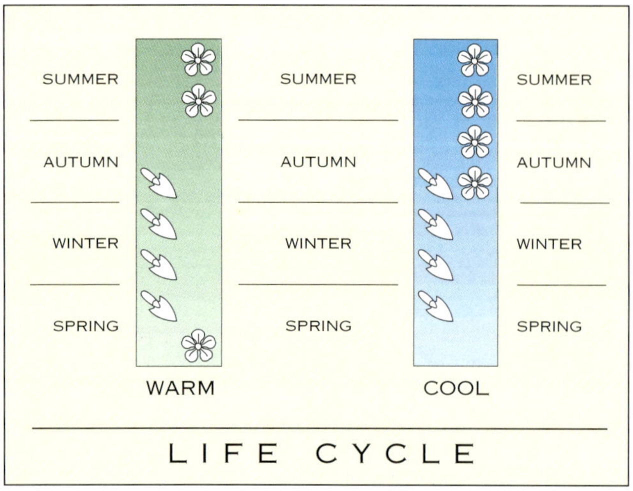

CONDITIONS

Climate Grows in cool or warm zones.

Aspect Prefers an open, sunny position all day.

Soil Performs best in well-drained soil enriched with organic matter but it will grow in poor soils too. Overrich soil may produce a profusion of foliage with poor flowering.

GROWING METHOD

Propagation Grows most easily from divisions of existing clumps lifted in late autumn, winter or early spring. Space new plants at about 30 cm intervals. Species can be grown from seed sown in autumn or early spring.

Watering Responds well to regular watering but is very drought tolerant.

Fertilising Apply complete plant food as growth begins in spring. However, no further fertilising should be needed.

Problems No pest or disease problems are known.

FLOWERING

Season The long flowering period extends through summer and autumn although some species bloom in spring.

Cutting Flowers can be cut for indoor decoration.

AFTER FLOWERING

Requirements Cut off spent flower stems and tidy up foliage as it dies back. In warm areas it may not die back completely.

CORYDALIS

Corydalis

THE FOLIAGE and flowers of Corydalis lutea *are both dainty and decorative. This adaptable species is worth trying in warmer areas.*

THE BLUE SPECIES and forms of corydalis are highly prized. This is Corydalis cashmeriana *with long, upcurving spurs on its flowers.*

FEATURES

Pretty, fern-like foliage and tubular, spurred flowers are characteristic of the 300 or so species of corydalis. Only a small number of species are grown in cultivation and most need to grow in areas with cold winters, although *C. lutea* and *C. ochroleuca* can be grown in warmer areas. Species in cultivation are mainly in shades of yellow or blue but there are some in pink or crimson. Some of the brilliant blues are highly sought after by gardeners in cool, moist districts, and a recent cultivar with electric blue flowers, known as 'Blue Panda', is widely available. Heights vary from 15 to 60 cm. Some corydalis are excellent rock garden plants, while others are suitable for mixed borders or planting under deciduous trees. Many varieties may be available only from specialist nurseries that concentrate on alpine or cool climate plants.

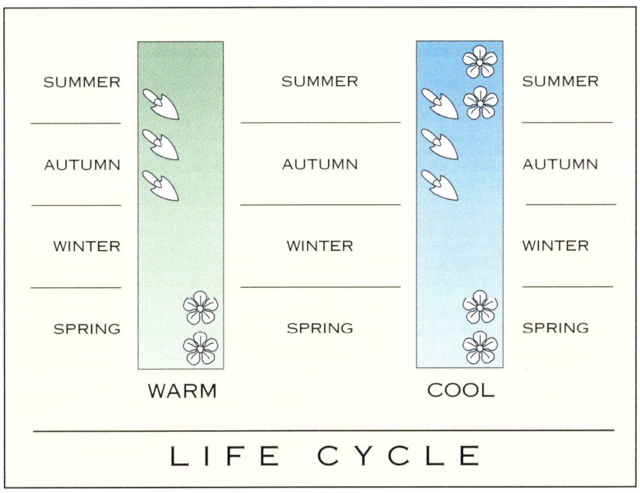

CONDITIONS

Climate Prefers a cool, moist climate but some can be tried in warmer areas.

Aspect The preferred aspect varies with the species. Some tolerate open, sunny spots in cool districts but others need dappled sunlight. Species tried in warm areas should be given plenty of shade.

Soil Needs very well-drained soil that is able to retain some moisture in summer.

GROWING METHOD

Propagation Grows from seed sown as soon as it is ripe, which is usually during summer. The seed is ripe when the small elongated capsules, which form after flowers have fallen, turn brown and dry. Some species can be divided while others produce tubers from which offsets can be divided. Plant out at 10–15 cm intervals.

Watering Needs regular watering in dry weather during spring and summer.

Fertilising Apply slow release fertiliser or a little blood and bone as growth commences in spring.

Problems There are no specific pest or disease problems.

FLOWERING

Season Most species flower in spring or from spring into summer.

Cutting The flowers are unsuitable for cutting.

AFTER FLOWERING

Requirements Remove spent flower stems unless you are waiting for seed to set. Tidy up foliage as it dies back.

CRANESBILL

Geranium species and cultivars

THE FOLIAGE on this cranesbill geranium is probably more decorative than the flowers, although the small blooms are certainly noticeable as they stand well clear of the plant.

THIS CRANESBILL with its stunning deep violet flowers blooms over a long period.

FEATURES

There are a great many perennial species of the true geranium, and many of them are reliable, long-flowering plants. Most cranesbill geraniums are easy to grow and they can be ideal in perennial borders, as edging plants or as infill planting between shrubs. Some species self-sow freely but unwanted seedlings are easily removed. Cranesbills range from about 15 cm to 1 m or so tall. Most have attractive, deeply divided leaves, and the flowers cover a range of shades, mostly in violet, blue, pink, rose and cerise. Species worth seeking out include *G. endressii* and its cultivars, especially 'Wargrave Pink', *G. pratense*, *G. psilostemon*, *G. himalayense* and *G. sanguineum*. A variety of *G. sanguineum* known as 'Lancastriense' is a dwarf-growing type that may be used as edging or groundcover. The plants most of us call geraniums are in fact pelargoniums.

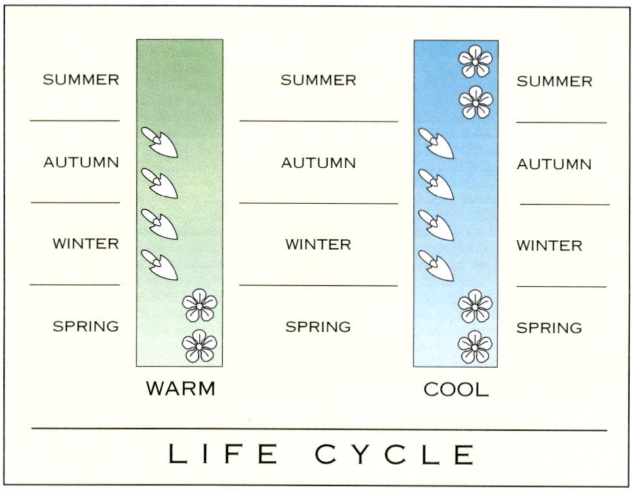

CONDITIONS

Climate Grows best in cool climates but some are worth trying in warm zones.

Aspect Prefers full sun.

Soil Needs open, well-drained soil but it need not be rich. Very acid soils should be limed before planting by adding about 100 g of lime or dolomite per square metre.

GROWING METHOD

Propagation Most cranesbills are easily grown from seed sown in autumn but results will be variable. They can also be grown from cuttings in the warmer months. Established clumps can be lifted and divided in late winter. Spacing depends on variety but is usually in the range of 20–40 cm.

Watering Established plants are fairly tolerant of dry conditions but benefit from deep watering in dry spring and summer weather.

Fertilising Apply a little complete plant food as growth starts in spring.

Problems No specific pest or disease problems are known for these plants.

FLOWERING

Season Cranesbills flower through spring and summer.

Cutting Flowers do not cut well.

AFTER FLOWERING

Requirements Remove spent flower stems unless you want plants to seed. Some pruning may be needed through the growing season if growth becomes too rampant.

DAYLILY

Hemerocallis species and hybrids

MAHOGANY RED is one of the many strong colours available in the huge range of daylily cultivars now available from specialist growers.

THE MASS PLANTING of this creamy yellow daylily increases its impact. Blooms will appear one after the other for many weeks.

FEATURES

Easily grown in a wide range of conditions, daylily is a trouble-free plant with single or double flowers. As its name suggests, individual flowers last only one day, but they are produced over a long period. They come in a wide range of colours, the main ones being shades of yellow, orange, red, magenta and purple. There is an enormous number of hybrids available from specialist growers. The clumps of grassy foliage may be from 25 cm to 1 m high; some are evergreen while others die down in winter.

While straight species are not as readily available as the hybrids, they are important in hybridising new varieties and several species are worth seeking out for themselves. They include *H. altissima* from China, which has pale yellow fragrant flowers on stems 1.5 m or so high; *H. aurantiaca*, which has orange flowers on stems to about 80 cm; and *H. lilio-asphodelus*, which has pale yellow fragrant flowers above leaves 50–60 cm high.

Categories Hemerocallis societies are active in some countries, especially in the United States. To help sort out the enormous number of cultivars they have put plants into categories such as evergreen, semi-evergreen or dormant (deciduous). This system is further refined according to the size of the plant—dwarf, medium or tall—and the expected flowering season, whether early, mid-season or late.

Dwarf forms The number of dwarf forms available is steadily increasing and they may be better suited to today's smaller gardens. Those with a reliable reflowering habit can also be successfully grown in pots. Use a good quality potting mix and crowd three plants into a 20 cm pot for good effect. 'Stella d'Oro' or 'Elf Caps' would be good ones to try.

Uses Mass plantings of dwarf or tall forms create the best effect. Daylilies are not plants that should be dotted about in the garden. Using a number of the one variety or at least the one colour is preferable to planting a mixture of types or colours. In a mixed border they give a very pleasing effect as the foliage is very full.

SMALLER VARIETIES of daylily bloom just as prolifically as the tall types but are easier to fit into a small garden scheme.

MANY OF the finest daylily cultivars are in creamy yellow or orange tones, not surprisingly as these are the colours of many of the species.

CONDITIONS

Climate Not suitable for the tropics but grows in any other climatic conditions.

Aspect Grows best in full sun but tolerates semi-shade in warm climates. Can be mass planted on banks or sloping ground as the roots are very efficient soil binders.

Soil Grows in any type of soil, wet or dry, but to get maximum growth from the newer hybrids the soil should be enriched with manure or compost before planting.

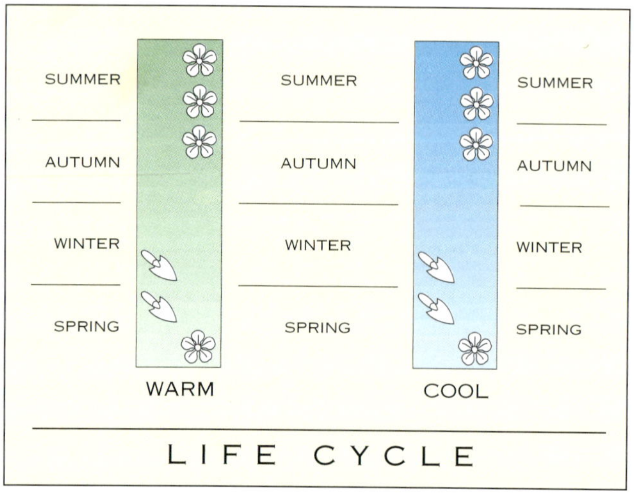

GROWING METHOD

Propagation Divide established clumps in late winter or very early spring. Cut back foliage before or straight after division. Spacing may be from 15 to 30 cm, depending on variety.

Watering Needs regular watering to establish. Once established plants are very drought tolerant but better sized blooms can be expected if deep waterings are given every week or two. Daylilies growing in very soggy ground tend to survive quite well but produce few flowers.

Fertilising Grows without supplementary fertiliser but an application of complete plant food in early spring encourages stronger growth.

Problems No specific problems are known.

FLOWERING

Season Depending on variety, plants may be in bloom any time from spring through until autumn. Many flower in late spring and early summer.

Cutting Flowers can be cut for the vase but they need to be renewed daily.

AFTER FLOWERING

Requirements Cut off spent flower stems. Herbaceous types that die down in autumn or early winter can have foliage cut back too.

DELPHINIUM

Delphinium elatum cultivars

DOZENS OF individual flowers make up the striking towers of delphinium flowers. Blue shades predominate in this plant.

THESE DELPHINIUMS, growing in the shelter of the house behind, should remain stately and upright throughout the flowering season.

FEATURES

Tall, handsome and stately, delphiniums are an outstanding feature of perennial borders in cool climates. In warmer areas they are mostly treated as annuals or biennials at most. Growing from 1 to 2 m high, the long-lasting spires of blooms originally came in a rich blue only but they now come in shades of pink, lavender and white, too. Delphiniums should be mass planted at the back of a border for the best effect but they can also be placed as accent plants in a border. Tall-growing varieties may need staking unless they are in a very sheltered spot. Colours can be mixed but the best effect comes from massing plants of the one colour. This delphinium is also cultivated as an annual in warmer areas.

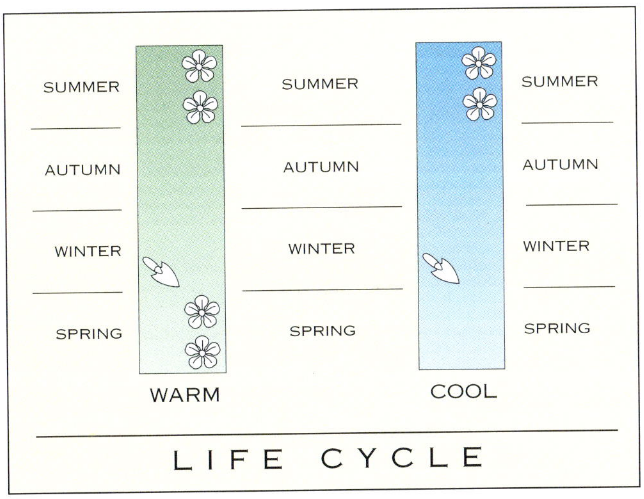

CONDITIONS

Climate Not suitable for the tropics or hot, arid areas. Grows as a perennial only in cool to cold areas.

Aspect Needs full sun and shelter from strong wind, and staking if not well sheltered.

Soil Needs well-drained soil enriched with copious amounts of decayed manure or compost before planting. Mulch established plants too.

GROWING METHOD

Propagation Divide established clumps in late winter, ensuring each division has a crown and its own roots. Space about 30 cm apart. Grows from seed sown in autumn but results are variable.

Watering Needs regular, deep watering throughout spring and summer.

Fertilising Apply complete plant food once growth begins in spring and each month until flowering.

Problems Watch for aphids on new growth and hose off or spray with pyrethrum or insecticidal soap. In humid conditions powdery mildew may need to be sprayed with a registered fungicide.

FLOWERING

Season Has a long blooming through summer or from mid-spring to early summer in warmer areas.

Cutting Flowers may be cut for the vase.

AFTER FLOWERING

Requirements Cut off flower stems once blooms have faded. Tidy plants as they die down in autumn.

DICHORISANDRA

Dichorisandra thyrsiflora

AN OUTSTANDING BEAUTY for the subtropics and tropics, dichorisandra flowers look rich blue or purple depending on the light.

LARGE CLUMPS of dichorisandra can be an outstanding feature of the garden, and they are trouble-free if grown in the right climate.

FEATURES

Growing well over 1 m high in good conditions, dichorisandra is an outstanding perennial for the warm climate garden as it enjoys high temperature and high humidity. It is, however, best grown in dappled sunlight under trees or under a pergola where it will not be exposed to midday sun. The rich royal blue to purple flowers are carried on tall spikes standing clear of the foliage and this plant always attracts great admiration when in flower. The foliage itself is a handsome glossy green. Dichorisandra is not especially fast growing but will eventually form a large clump, expanding on its short rhizomes. It could also be grown in a container. This plant is easy to grow and long lived if it is grown in the right environment.

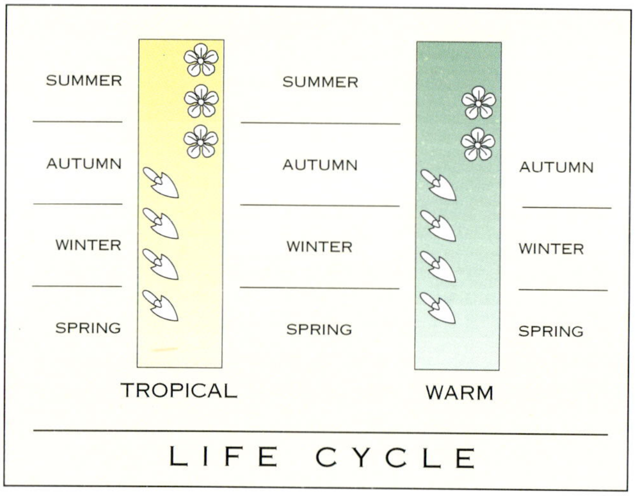

CONDITIONS

Climate Grows best in the tropics and subtropics but can be grown in warm, frost-free areas.

Aspect Likes a sheltered position in partial shade.

Soil Soil should be heavily enriched with compost or manure and should drain well. Mulch plants with decayed compost or manure, too.

GROWING METHOD

Propagation Grows from seed sown in spring but is most easily propagated from stem cuttings taken in autumn or early spring or by divisions of the fleshy roots in late winter. Space plants 25–30 cm apart.

Watering Needs an abundant supply of water throughout spring and summer.

Fertilising Apply blood and bone or complete plant food in spring.

Problems There are no specific pest or disease problems.

FLOWERING

Season The brilliant blue to purple flower spikes are carried over a fairly long period through summer into autumn.

Cutting Flowers could be cut for the house but will give better value in the garden.

AFTER FLOWERING

Requirements Remove spent flower stems unless you want seed to ripen. If clumps become congested, some of the older canes can be cut out at ground level.

DIETES

Dietes bicolor, D. grandiflora

THE SYMMETRY of the Dietes bicolor *flower makes it worthy of a closer look. The yellow petals and brown markings are quite distinctive.*

THE SWORD-LIKE foliage and dainty flowers of Dietes grandiflora *are here seen at their best, silhouetted against a wall.*

FEATURES

Dietes has been widely planted in large-scale landscaping projects because of its ability to cope with poor conditions and almost total neglect. However, it is also a useful home garden plant, providing good foliage effects as well as the decorative flowers. Foliage is upright, stiff and sword shaped, growing to around 1 m high. The flowers, which are iris-like, are pale yellow with a brownish blotch on *D. bicolor*, while *D. grandiflora* has white flowers with yellow markings and mauve-blue styles for a pretty effect. Dietes can be planted in bold clumps or singly as foliage contrast among other, softer looking plants. It is a good soil binder for planting on banks and is ideal for areas where water is scarce.

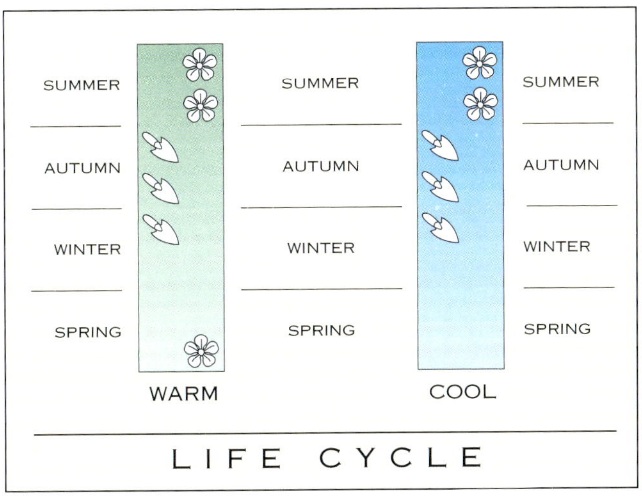

CONDITIONS

Climate Grows from cool to subtropical regions.

Aspect Grows best in full sun but tolerates shade, although flowering may not be as profuse in shaded situations.

Soil Needs well-drained soil. It need not be rich.

GROWING METHOD

Propagation Grows easily from seed sown in late summer or autumn, or from divisions of existing clumps. Clumps are best divided in autumn or early winter. Replant divisions about 30 cm apart.

Watering Once established, this is very drought tolerant but plants will look better if given occasional deep watering in dry weather.

Fertilising Supplementary feeding is not essential but improved growth will result if plants are given complete plant food in early spring.

Problems No specific pest or disease problems are known for dietes.

FLOWERING

Season Flowering is from late spring throughout the summer months.

Cutting Dietes do not make good cut flowers.

AFTER FLOWERING

Requirements It is best to do nothing after flowering as the same stems continue to flower over quite a few years. Remove old brown leaves or flower stems that you consider unsightly.

EASTER DAISY

Aster

ABUNDANT FLOWERS almost totally obscure the foliage on this Easter daisy.

THIS IS Aster ericoides, *considered by many to be the true Easter daisy.*

ONE OF the best red Easter daisies is the low-growing 'Winston Churchill'.

FEATURES

There is a large variety of Easter, or Michaelmas, daisies grown, and all of them flower in late summer and autumn. The most commonly grown is *A. novi-belgii*, which has a range of cultivars from dwarf forms 25 cm high to tall varieties growing up to 1 m. Flowers are blue, violet, pink, red or white and all are good for cutting. *A. ericoides* has very small leaves but produces stems of white flowers up to 1 m high—this is probably the species most usually known as Easter daisy. *A.* x *frikartii* grows about 75 cm high and has violet-blue flowers. These plants are all extremely easy to grow and tolerate a wide range of conditions. They multiply readily, too, so that large clumps are soon built up.

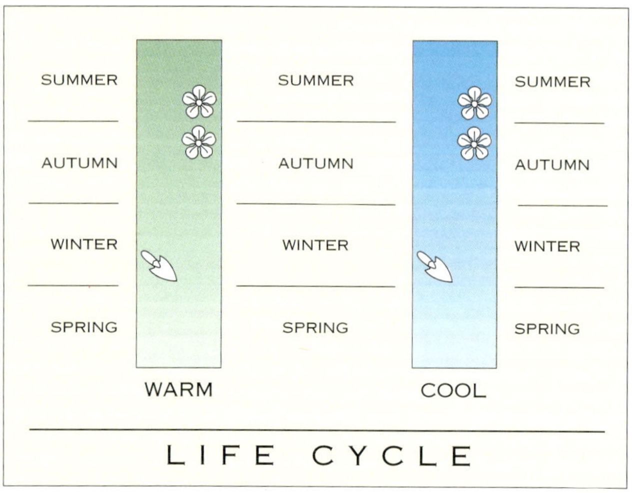

CONDITIONS

Climate Suitable for cool or warm regions only.

Aspect Grows best in full sun. Tolerates light shade but blooming may not be so prolific and growth will be less compact.

Soil Needs well-drained soil but it does not need rich soil.

GROWING METHOD

Propagation Divide clumps in late winter. These plants are prolific growers and one plant will multiply itself at least tenfold in a season. Replant divisions at least 20 cm apart.

Watering Best results are from heavy, regular watering during spring and summer. However, they will tolerate long dry periods well.

Fertilising Apply complete plant food in early spring as growth begins.

Problems No specific problems are known.

FLOWERING

Season The long flowering display lasts from late summer into autumn.

Cutting Cut flowers last very well if given frequent water changes.

AFTER FLOWERING

Requirements Cut off spent flower stems close to ground level after blooming. Plants will gradually die back but should not need any more attention until late winter or spring.

GAURA
Gaura lindheimeri

GAURA FLOWERS can appear to be floating on their long slender stems, while the long stamens add to the impression of airiness.

NATURAL-LOOKING meadow-type plantings can be difficult to achieve in a garden but a mass planting of gaura will be helpful.

FEATURES

This herbaceous perennial, which hails from the southern United States, is very easy to grow and gives great value in the garden. It is in flower for many months of the year. Flowering stems that may be up to 1.2 m tall emerge from a cluster of basal leaves. The dainty white flowers on slender stems have a pink calyx producing a pretty pink and white effect. This plant suits the cottage garden style very well and is a good mainstay in a mixed border. In a large garden it can be mass planted to good effect or repeated as an accent plant throughout the garden. New plantings should be spaced no less than 50 cm apart. It sometimes self-seeds but plants are readily moved if they pop up in the wrong place.

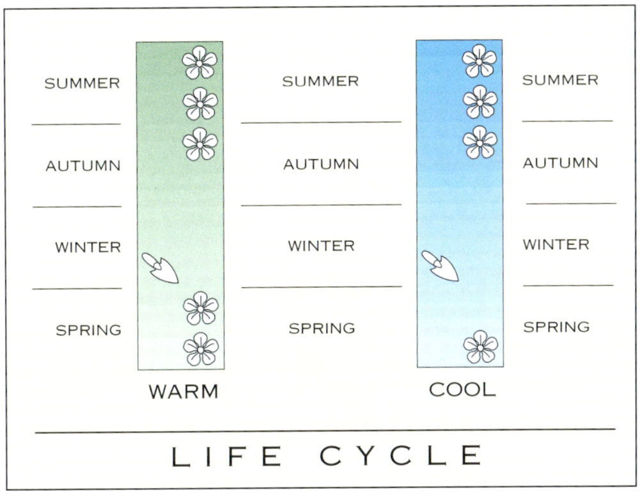

CONDITIONS

Climate Grows in both cool and warm regions and the subtropics.

Aspect Prefers an open position in full sun.

Soil Needs well-drained soil but it need not be rich, although plants respond well to soil enriched with organic matter.

GROWING METHOD

Propagation Divide existing clumps in late winter—they usually multiply well. Gaura can also be grown from seed sown from early spring through to autumn.

Watering Although tolerant of dry conditions, these plants respond well to occasional deep watering during dry weather in the spring and summer months.

Fertilising Apply complete plant food in early spring.

Problems Gaura is usually trouble free but is occasionally affected by a fungal leaf spot in very humid, warm weather. Treatment is not usually necessary.

FLOWERING

Season The very long flowering period is from spring, through summer and sometimes into autumn.

Cutting Flowers are unsuitable for cutting.

AFTER FLOWERING

Requirements Prune off spent flower stems. As growth dies back cut off all the old growth to ground level.

GAZANIA

Gazania species and hybrids

THIS HYBRID GAZANIA shows complex patterns at the centre of the petals.

EXCELLENT GROUNDCOVERS and soil binders, gazanias tolerate most conditions while providing a welcome splash of colour, as these vigorous yellow plants show.

FEATURES

This evergreen, easy-care plant is very tough and able to grow in the most inhospitable conditions. Growing 15–20 cm high, it tolerates poor, dry soil and exposure to salt wind. It is a great soil binder and is frequently used to hold soil on banks or to stop sand drift in seaside areas. One plant may eventually spread to 50 cm. It makes an attractive edging plant and it can also be grown in containers. The species *G. rigens* has yellow or orange flowers with a dark centre but there are many outstanding hybrids. There is an amazing range of brilliant colours ranging from soft pastel pinks and cream through to strong reds and mahogany. Some of the two-toned or three-toned striped varieties are really eye-catching. All have pretty contrasting centres.

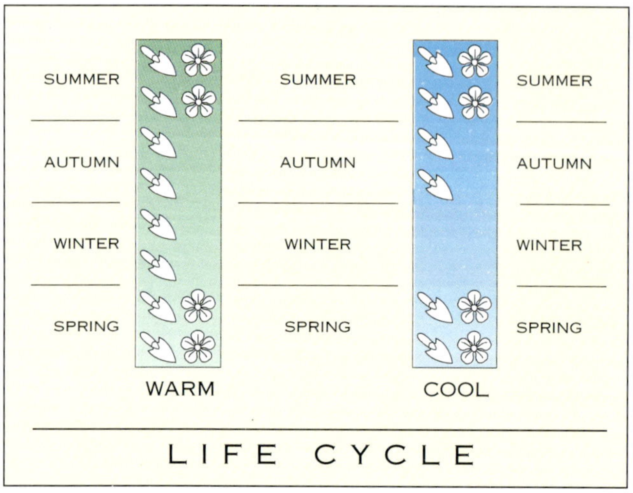

CONDITIONS

Climate Suitable for warm to subtropical regions, including arid areas. Grows well in exposed coastal conditions.

Aspect Must have full sun all day for best results.

Soil Needs well-drained soil that is not rich. Soils rich in organic matter usually hold too much water for gazanias.

GROWING METHOD

Propagation Grows easily from division of established clumps at most times of the year. Cuttings make roots readily through most of the year. Average planting intervals are usually about 20 cm.

Watering Water regularly to establish. Once plants are growing well, give only a very occasional deep watering in prolonged dry periods.

Fertilising Feed lightly with blood and bone sometime during early spring.

Problems There are no problems if gazanias are grown in the right conditions.

FLOWERING

Season The long flowering period lasts throughout spring into early summer and at times may extend even longer.

Cutting Flowers are not suitable for cutting.

AFTER FLOWERING

Requirements Cut off spent flower stems but no other pruning is necessary.

GERANIUM
Pelargonium x hortorum

*IVY-LEAF GERANIUM (*Pelargonium peltatum*) grows to cover a large area. Culture is the same as for other geraniums.*

BRIGHT RED GERANIUMS are used to unify this garden, the pots on the edge of the deck echoing those on the fence line below.

FEATURES

One of several plants commonly known as geraniums, this is the soft-wooded evergreen geranium also known as the zonal geranium or pelargonium. It grows from about 30 to 60 cm high and has a rounded, shrubby habit. The soft leaves have a rounded form with lobed edges and the leaf is marked in concentric zones in a horseshoe shape. Some varieties have very decorative and colourful foliage but most of these have insignificant flowers. Most geraniums, however, are grown for their flowers, which are borne in rounded heads made up of many individual flowers. There are singles, doubles and some with rosebud form. The colour range is extensive, from white through pink, red, apricot, lavender and magenta, plus those that are striped in two tones or contrasting colours.

Uses This geranium is an old garden favourite but it is also well loved as a potted plant. In cooler climates where plants grow more slowly and don't become rangy, they make ideal edging plants. A garden bed edged with geraniums all in one colour can add structure to any garden, whether the planting behind them is formal or very informal.

CONDITIONS

Climate Prefers hot and warm climates. In cool climates this plant needs protection during winter and it may need to be overwintered in frost-free conditions.

Aspect For the best results grow geranium in full sun all day.

Soil Needs very free-draining soil. Acid soils should be limed before planting by the addition of about 100 g of lime or dolomite per square metre.

GROWING METHOD

Propagation Tip cuttings about 10 cm long strike easily at almost any time of year. Plant them out at least 20 cm apart.

Watering Needs regular watering until it is well established but once geranium is established it can withstand drought. It is always better to underwater geraniums rather than overwater them, as this can result in more foliage and fewer flowers.

Fertilising Apply slow release fertiliser or pelletted poultry manure as growth starts during the spring months.

HARDY PINK AND RED GERANIUMS are used to brighten the driveway on this steeply sloping site. They look very effective cascading over the stone wall, providing contrast in colour and size with the dainty erigeron growing along the base of the wall.

Problems There are few disease problems if plants are growing in the right conditions but rust, a fungal disease, is very common in warm, humid weather. Pick off the worst affected leaves, and try to avoid watering late in the day. Overhead watering should also be avoided as the splashes will help spread the rust spores. Caterpillars can do a lot of damage and may be hard to locate. Remove them by hand if possible or spray plants with the bioinsecticide *Bacillus thuringiensis*.

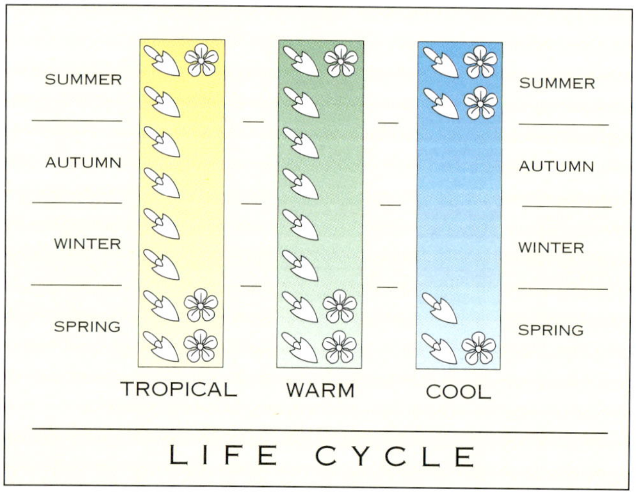

FLOWERING

Season The main flowering is through spring into early summer but geraniums will spot flower through the warmer months and will give a second flush in late summer or autumn if they are cut back and fed lightly after the main spring flowering is over.

Cutting Flowers do not pick well.

AFTER FLOWERING

Requirements Cut off spent flower heads. The whole plant should be pruned back hard when flowering has finished, in early to mid-autumn.

POTTED GERANIUMS

Maintenance Potted geraniums feature widely in Mediterranean gardens and they are a favourite plant for window boxes and planters in Europe. They have no real problems there but if you are growing them in humid climates where the fungal disease rust is a problem, make sure that the pots are placed in full sun and that there is plenty of space around them to ensure good air circulation. Avoid overhead watering wherever possible and be careful not to overwater plants.

GERBERA

Gerbera jamesonii

PERFECT FLOWERS such as these are almost unattainable in the home garden but gerberas can look marvellous even when imperfect.

OLDER VARIETIES and species gerberas are reliable and prolific flowerers. These salmon ones blend beautifully with white candytuft.

FEATURES

Also known as Transvaal daisy, evergreen gerbera gives a long garden display. The species has ray flowers in red or orange but many modern hybrids have single or double rows of ray florets in many shades of pink, salmon, red or yellow. Some of the very large fancy types seen in florists' shops are generally not available to the home gardener and others may be had only through specialist mail-order nurseries. Flower stems rise up to 50 cm from the lobed basal leaves and plants eventually form large clumps. They are best grown at the front of a border or massed in groups through the garden. They can also be grown in pots.

CONDITIONS

Climate Grows in warm and tropical districts. Gerbera has no frost tolerance.

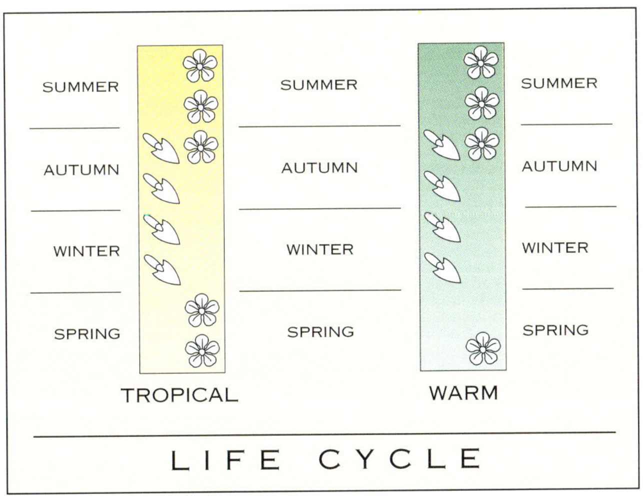

Aspect Needs full sun all day for best results.

Soil Needs very well-drained soil. If drainage is doubtful, plant in raised beds. Decayed organic matter can be added to the soil well ahead of planting time.

GROWING METHOD

Propagation Divide established clumps in autumn or late winter. Species gerberas will grow from ripe seed collected when petals have fallen and the flower disc is starting to disintegrate. Space plants about 40 cm or so apart to give clumps room to spread. It is essential to plant gerberas with the crown above soil level.

Watering Water regularly in spring and summer but keep fairly dry during autumn and winter.

Fertilising Apply complete plant food in spring and light dressings every few weeks when in flower.

Problems Plants can be killed by crown or root rot if planted too deeply or if drainage is poor. Fungal leaf spots and white rust may affect foliage. Pick off the worst leaves, avoid overhead watering and spray with a fungicide if necessary. Greening and distortion of flowers is caused by big bud or virescence, a disease carried by sap-sucking leafhoppers. There is no cure for this disease.

FLOWERING

Season Flowers may be produced from mid-spring until autumn if regularly dead-headed.

Cutting Excellent for the vase if cut when first fully open but scald stems before arranging.

AFTER FLOWERING

Requirements Remove spent flower stems and dead foliage.

GEUM

Geum quellyon, syn. *G. coccineum*

THE BRIGHT RED double geum 'Mrs Bradshaw' deserves its popularity.

LIKE MOST PERENNIALS, geums look best when planted together in large numbers. Here a mass of deep red flowers looks wonderful against a background of green foliage.

FEATURES

Although there are many species of geum, the two most commonly grown are cultivars of this species. 'Lady Stratheden' has double yellow flowers and 'Mrs Bradshaw' bright scarlet double flowers. If you are in a cool area there are other good forms it is worth seeking out. Flowers appear on stems 30–50 cm high that emerge from large rosettes of slightly hairy, lobed compound leaves. Foliage is generally evergreen but may be herbaceous in some areas. Geums can be planted as accent plants, preferably in groups, in the garden or near the front of a mixed border. While flowers are not very suitable for cutting, they give a long display in the garden if they are regularly dead-headed.

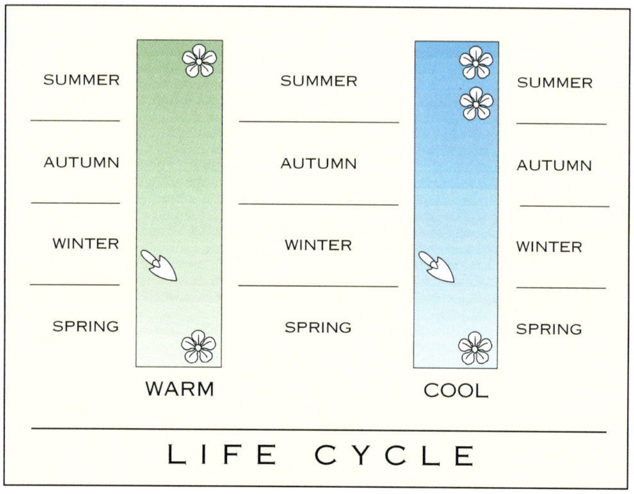

CONDITIONS

Climate Grows best in cooler regions although it is worth trying in warm areas.

Aspect Prefers full sun but can also be grown in semi-shade, especially in warmer areas.

Soil Needs well-drained soil and plants will benefit from the addition of plenty of decayed manure or compost before planting.

GROWING METHOD

Propagation Clumps can be divided in late winter. Cut back foliage to reduce moisture loss while divisions re-establish. Also grows from seed sown in spring but plants may not be true to type. Plant about 25–30 cm apart.

Watering Needs regular, deep watering in dry weather during spring and summer. Does not tolerate drying out in the growing season.

Fertilising Apply complete plant food in early spring and again in midsummer.

Problems No particular problems are known.

FLOWERING

Season There is a long flowering display through late spring and summer.

Cutting Regular cutting (or dead-heading) is essential to prolong the display.

AFTER FLOWERING

Requirements None apart from the removal of spent flower stems and any dead foliage under the rosette.

GLOBE THISTLE

Echinops

THESE METALLIC BLUE globe thistles form an elegant picture against a stone wall.

EARLY MORNING LIGHT accentuates the rounded, slightly spiky heads of these globe thistle flowers, planted here in a bold drift in a country garden.

FEATURES

This is a very distinctive-looking plant that makes a good accent in a mixed planting. Taller species need to be placed at the back of a border but others can be planted in bold groups through the bed. Most have foliage that is stiff, prickly and finely divided, with silvery stems growing from 30 cm to almost 2 m. Some of the species have foliage that is covered with fine white hairs on the underside. The flower heads are usually white or metallic blue and are highly prized for their decorative value when cut and dried. Probably the most commonly grown is *E. ritro* and its cultivars, some of which have deep blue flowers. *E. sphaerocephalus* has pale grey to silvery flowers. This is a herbaceous perennial that will survive and thrive in poor soils.

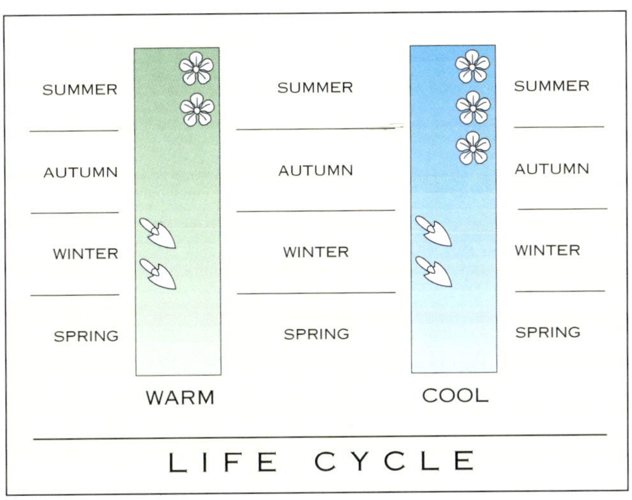

CONDITIONS

Climate Grows in cool to warm regions.

Aspect Prefers full sun all day.

Soil Soil must be very well drained but need not be rich. Globe thistle can be grown in poor, gravelly or sandy soils.

GROWING METHOD

Propagation Grow it from seed, from division of existing clumps or from root cuttings. All propagation is done in winter. Plant out about 40 cm apart.

Watering Water regularly to establish. Although drought tolerant, this plant benefits from occasional deep watering during dry spring and summer weather.

Fertilising Apply complete plant food or poultry manure in early spring.

Problems There are no known pest or disease problems but plants will rot if overwatered or if soil is poorly drained.

FLOWERING

Season There is a long flowering period through summer into autumn.

Cutting Flower heads required for drying should be cut before the blooms are fully open.

AFTER FLOWERING

Requirements Cut off any remaining spent flower heads unless you want the seed to ripen. As the plant dies down, clean away dead foliage. A rosette of leaves may persist in warmer districts.

GOLDEN TUFT

Aurinia saxatilis*, syn. *Alyssum saxatile

SUNNY YELLOW FLOWERS and the rather dull green foliage of golden tuft are in sharp contrast, making the flowers very prominent.

YELLOW AND BLUE are always a fashionable colour combination, and this planting of golden tuft and Italian lavender shows why.

FEATURES

This is a little, rounded, evergreen perennial that may grow from 10 to 30 cm high, forming a mound up to 40 or 50 cm across. In the species the flowers are a clear yellow but the various cultivars of this plant produce flowers that may be white, cream, lemon or rich gold. Its natural habitat is rocky, mountainous country so it is ideal for a rock garden, for planting on dry, sloping ground or for edging garden beds as long as the drainage is good. It is also ideally suited to planting in troughs or around the edges of large pots that perhaps contain a shrub or small tree. Although golden tuft is a perennial, some gardeners grow it as part of their spring annual display.

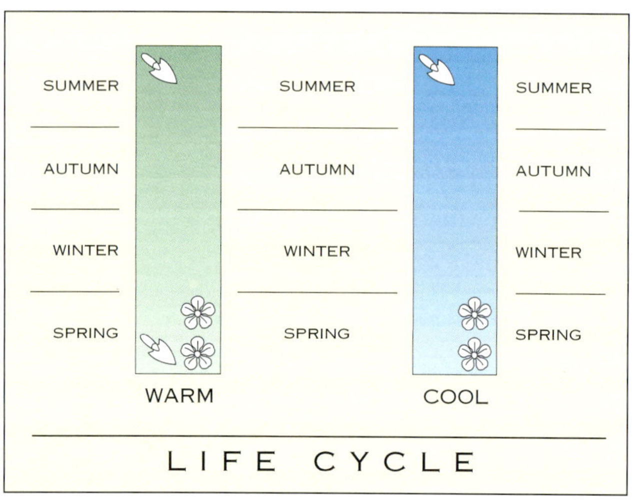

CONDITIONS

Climate Prefers a cool climate but is worth trying in warm zones.

Aspect Needs an open position in full sun.

Soil Soil must be very free draining but it need not be rich.

GROWING METHOD

Propagation Grows readily from seed sown in late summer. Cultivars can be grown from tip cuttings taken in late spring and early summer. Space plants about 10 cm apart.

Watering In dry spring and summer weather give deep watering, perhaps every week to ten days.

Fertilising Small amounts only of complete plant food may be given in early spring but fertilising is not essential.

Problems No specific problems are known but poor drainage or overwatering can kill these plants.

FLOWERING

Season Flowers appear from middle to late spring, the flowers completely covering the plant and hiding the foliage.

Cutting These flowers are not suitable for picking.

AFTER FLOWERING

Requirements It is probably easiest to shear over the whole plant with clippers unless you are waiting for seed to ripen. Shearing plants helps to keep them compact and rounded in form.

GUNNERA
Gunnera manicata

MASSIVE LEAVES ensure gunneras will be the dominant feature of most plantings.

DAMP GROUND at the bottom of this bank allows the clump of gunnera really to thrive. The lovely pink-flowering shrub beside it is a hawthorn (Crataegus *species).*

FEATURES

This is not a plant for small gardens. Growing to 2.5 m high, clumps may grow 3–4 m wide. The huge rhubarb-like leaves can be well over a metre in diameter and are supported by long, stout, hairy stems. This is a magnificent feature plant for wet areas of a garden, beside a pond or stream or on the edge of a lawn. In early summer it produces a tall spike of greenish flowers, often completely concealed by the foliage, but this plant is grown for the impact of its giant foliage. It is herbaceous, dying right back to the ground in winter. This is not a difficult plant to grow in the right conditions but it must be carefully sited.

CONDITIONS

Climate Prefers a cool climate. It occurs naturally in areas that are cool, wet and fairly frost-free.

Aspect Grows in semi-shade or sun in cool areas.

Soil Likes a rich, moist soil. Dig plenty of organic matter into the soil before planting and mulch crowns heavily with decayed compost or manure for protection.

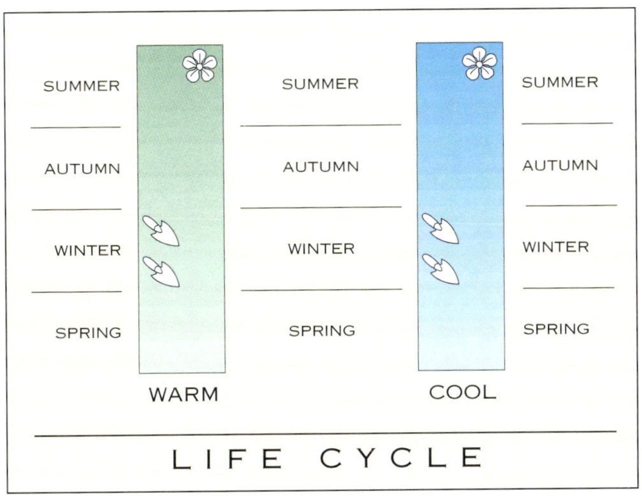

GROWING METHOD

Propagation Divide existing clumps in late winter, replanting them no less than 2 m apart. Cuttings can be taken from new growth, too. Pot them up and nurture them until they are well rooted. Plants can be raised from seed but this is slow and difficult.

Watering Keep moist throughout spring and summer.

Fertilising Apply blood and bone or pelletted poultry manure as growth commences in early spring. Add some fresh mulch of rotted manure at the same time.

Problems No specific pest or disease problems are known for gunnera.

FLOWERING

Season Heavy spikes of greenish flowers are produced in early summer.

Fruits The inflorescence is followed by fleshy red-green fruits, which can be ornamental.

AFTER FLOWERING

Requirements As weather becomes cold in autumn and leaves begin to brown, cut off foliage and cover the crown of the plant with a thick layer of straw and dry leaves to prevent it freezing. This cover should remain in place until frost-free weather the following spring, as hard frost after the leaves begin to emerge in spring causes burning.

Gymea Lily

Doryanthes excelsa

THE INTRICATE BEAUTY and delicate rosy colour of the Gymea lily flower is often lost to sight as it is so far up in the air.

GYMEA LILY needs plenty of room to grow as the stiff, sword-like foliage will, in time, produce a massive clump.

FEATURES

Also known as spear lily or torch lily, this is an evergreen perennial which is a truly magnificent sight in flower. The flower head consists of a dense cluster of deep red flowers that open to reveal a rich rosy pink. The flower spike rises 4 m or more from a large clump of broad, strappy leaves. Individual leaves may be up to 20 cm wide and an established clump of this plant may be 2 m or more high and the same across. This can be excellent as a feature plant in the garden or as the focal point of a mixed planting. If space allows, it looks wonderful planted in groups of three or more plants spaced at least 1.5 m apart. A closely related species, *D. palmeri*, has similar foliage but is a slightly larger plant and the flower spike tends to arch out sideways.

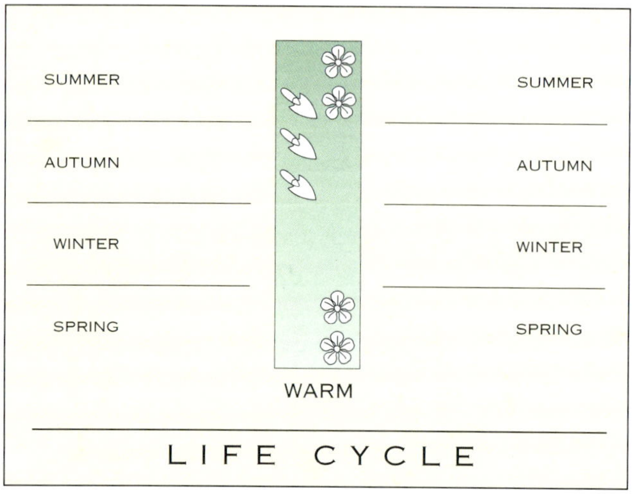

CONDITIONS

Climate Grows best in warm and subtropical zones. Frost tends to burn flower buds.

Aspect Prefers full sun but can be grown in dappled sunlight.

Soil Needs very well-drained soil but the soil need not be rich.

GROWING METHOD

Propagation Grows most easily from seed sown in late summer and autumn. Division of clumps is extremely difficult. Large clumps need to be machine dug and lifted.

Watering Established plants are fairly drought tolerant but growth will be best if plants are given deep watering at least every couple of weeks in dry spring and summer weather.

Fertilising Use only slow release granular fertiliser around these plants. They can be mulched with well-decayed compost or very old manure.

Problems There are no specific pest or disease problems.

FLOWERING

Season Main flowering is in spring but it can flower in summer.

Cutting As cut flowers these are spectacular but the flowers last much longer on the plant.

AFTER FLOWERING

Requirements Cut off the spent flower stalk after flowering or leave it until the seed has ripened. This may take several months.

Honey Flower

Melianthus major

NECTAR-RICH, these dark red flowers are very attractive to insects. The foliage, too, is unusual, with its distinctive colour and form.

THE BLUE-GREEN FOLIAGE of honey flower is a feature in itself. Only in a large garden will you get the full effect.

FEATURES

This very striking evergreen plant with its unusual blue-green foliage really stands out among other plants. It is grown as a feature in a mixed border or as a focal point in an annual or perennial display. In a large garden it could be repeat planted to tie together various parts of the garden. Honey flower can grow to over 2 m in height and it spreads by suckers, forming a large clump if left undivided. The dark mahogany-red flowers contain copious quantities of nectar very attractive to bees, giving the plant its common name. Although native to South Africa, it has become naturalised in India and some other warm areas of the world. In cool regions the top growth will be destroyed by frost but it can be grown if the root area is well protected during winter.

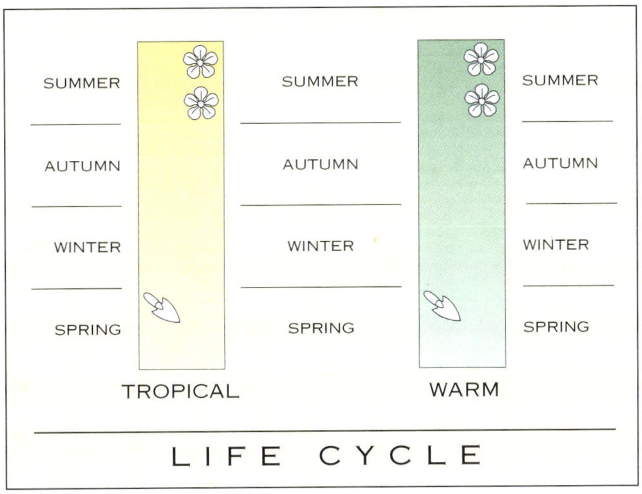

CONDITIONS

Climate Grows most easily in tropical and warm zones. It can be grown in cool areas if ample winter protection is provided.

Aspect Needs full sun all day.

Soil Soil must be well drained but it need not be rich. Enriched soils will produce good foliage effects but poor flowering. However, the outstanding foliage is the main reason for growing this plant.

GROWING METHOD

Propagation Grows from seed sown in spring or from division of suckers on an existing plant, also in spring. Plant at least 1 m apart.

Watering For best growth give deep watering every week or two in the growing season. It will, however, tolerate drought well.

Fertilising Apply complete plant food in spring for good foliage growth.

Problems No specific problems are known.

FLOWERING

Season Flowers are produced in summer.

Cutting Flowers are probably best left on the plant as they do not smell particularly pleasant.

AFTER FLOWERING

Requirements Cut off the spent flower stems unless you are waiting for seed to set and ripen. In cool areas cover the root area thickly with mulch to protect it from frost.

Hosta

Hosta species and hybrids

LEAVES PATTERNED VARIOUSLY in lime-green and blue make this hybrid hosta an outstanding garden ornament. Here it lights up a dull area under a tree, the little available light being reflected outwards by the lime-green. In shady areas where few flowers bloom, it can be a real boon.

FEATURES

SUMMER AUTUMN WINTER SPRING

HERBACEOUS

Also known as plantain lily, this herbaceous perennial is grown for its very decorative foliage. It is long lived and foliage may be tiny or have leaves up to 30 cm wide and 45 cm high. There are hundreds of cultivars with leaves that may be light or dark green, chartreuse or yellow, grey-green or blue. Many are variegated. Leaf texture also varies: it can be smooth or shiny, matt or powdery, puckered or corrugated. Hostas form clumps that create weed-free areas as they grow larger and more dense but the area around them should be kept mulched and weed-free until they emerge. Hostas look best mass planted near water features or when allowed to multiply in shady areas under trees.

Variegations Cultivars with cream, white or yellow variegations will light up a shady part of the garden, and as long as the tree or shrub canopy is high enough to let sufficient light reach the hostas, they will maintain their variegation. Likewise plants with sharp chartreuse or acid-lime coloured foliage can be used to give a lift to shaded areas. Types can be mixed to create a wealth of different effects, but unless your garden is very large, a few types may be best.

Flowers The bell-shaped flowers, mostly in mauve shades, appear in late spring to early summer and are held high above the foliage. Some species such as *H. plantaginea* and its cultivar 'Grandiflora' produce pure white, lightly fragrant flowers. However, few people plant hostas for the sake of their flowers, which are incidental to the wonderful effects that can be created with the foliage.

Companions Hostas do not come into leaf early in spring and so early flowering bulbs, such as snowdrops or snowflakes, or early perennials such as coydalis can be planted among them. These plants make a show right at the beginning of spring, if not late winter, and are past their best when hostas leaf out.

CONDITIONS

Climate Suitable for cool to warm areas only. Only a few species are truly suited to warm areas.

Aspect Needs shade or dappled sunlight. Grows in more open spots in very cool zones. Blue-leaved forms can be hardest of all to place as they turn green with too much sun or in heavy shade. Yellow or gold forms need some direct sun in early morning or very late afternoon.

PURE WHITE FLOWERS appear on some species of hosta such as Hosta plantaginea *and some of its cultivars.*

STRONGLY PUCKERED LEAVES in a bluish colour and white flowers are characteristic of Hosta sieboldiana *'Elegans'.*

HOSTAS, RODGERSIAS and ferns revel in the light shade and constant damp soil prevalent in woodlands.

Soil Needs rich and moisture-retentive soil. Large amounts of decayed manure or compost should be dug into the planting area well before planting. Mulch plants well after planting.

GROWING METHOD

Propagation The fleshy underground rhizomes can be divided in late winter. Most hostas are best divided only every four or five years. Plant dwarf cultivars 10–15 cm apart, large growers at least 70 cm apart.

Watering Must be kept moist and well watered throughout spring and summer.

Fertilising Apply pelletted poultry manure or blood and bone as growth begins in spring.

Problems Slugs and snails cause tremendous damage to hostas. Search for snails, use baits if you don't have a dog, and avoid watering in the evening.

FLOWERING

Season Flowers are produced in late spring or summer. Colour varies from white to purple.

Cutting Hosta can be used as a cut flower but flowers are not especially long lasting.

AFTER FLOWERING

Requirements Cut off any spent flower stems. Continue watering the plants until the foliage begins to die down and then tidy up the clumps. Mulch the area with compost or manure to keep it damp and weed-free during the time the plants are dormant.

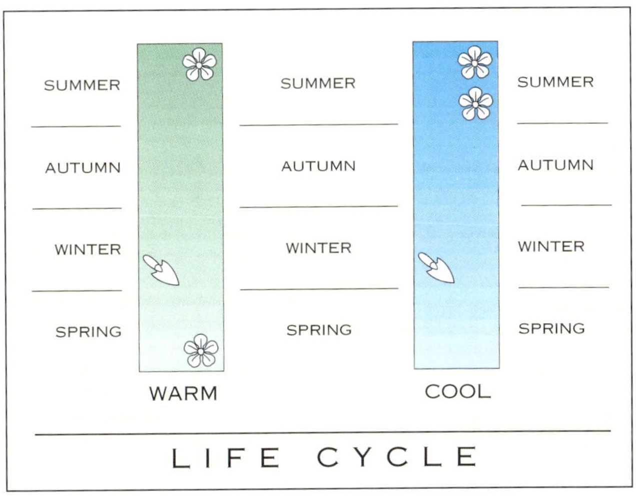

Hot Water Plant

Achimenes species and hybrids

HOT CERISE PINK flowers decorate this pretty little plant throughout summer. Hot water plants come in a range of colours.

SUMMER FOLIAGE is profuse and appears quickly once the weather is warm. It dies back and disappears during its dormant season.

FEATURES

HERBACEOUS

Hot water plant is in the same family as African violet and gloxinia and has richly coloured flowers in shades of purple, mauve, pink, red and cerise. This herbaceous perennial may grow from 15 to 50 cm high and spread 30 cm or so. It has a long flowering period through summer into autumn. Hot water plant is ideal for growing in hanging baskets or pots but can also be grown in the garden in a warm, sheltered spot as long as it does not get too wet during the dormant winter period. The foliage is attractive, too, the undersides of the leaves having a reddish tint. This is a very easy-care plant for a warm climate as long as it is not overwatered. It came by its common name because it needs to be started in warm conditions, such as in a glasshouse or near the hot water pipes in cold climates.

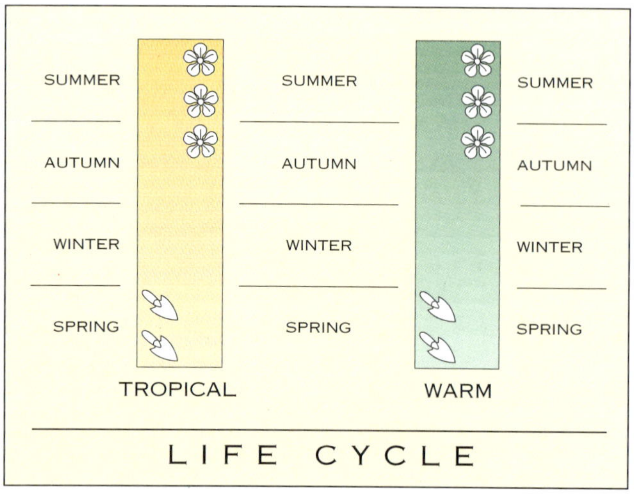

CONDITIONS

Climate Suitable for growing outdoors in tropical and warm zones only. In cooler areas it is grown in glasshouses or conservatories.

Aspect Grows in sun or semi-shade.

Soil Soil must be very well drained and rich in organic matter. For container growing use a good quality potting mix.

GROWING METHOD

Propagation The brittle tuberous rhizomes can be cut and replanted immediately in spring, being spaced at 10–15 cm intervals. Container-grown plants are best left undisturbed until they are very crowded.

Watering Needs regular watering during its active growing period but the soil should never be soggy. Keep dry during the dormant stage.

Fertilising Apply liquid fertiliser or blood and bone when growth begins in spring.

Problems No specific problems are known apart from rotting due to overwatering.

FLOWERING

Season There is a long flowering period through summer and autumn.

Cutting Flowers are not suitable for cutting.

AFTER FLOWERING

Requirements Tidy up plants as growth dies down. Stop watering once foliage starts to die down. Plants grown in the garden may need protection from heavy rain.

JACOB'S LADDER

Polemonium caeruleum

THE SKY-BLUE FLOWERS of Jacob's ladder are short lived in warm areas but appear for a long period in its preferred climate.

DELICATE FOLIAGE gives Jacob's ladder a fern-like appearance and yet it grows in sunnier spots than ferns would like.

FEATURES

The foliage on this pretty plant is somewhat fern-like and the clear sky-blue flowers usually last from late spring through summer. Plants can grow up to 1 m high but are usually half this size. Jacob's ladder is a favourite for a cottage garden but it can also be a useful addition to any mixed perennial or annual planting. For best effect mass plants together, planting them about 20 cm apart. They can be container grown, too. Native to northern and central Europe and northern Asia, this plant occurs naturally in both damp grasslands and rocky soils. It grows from a creeping rhizome (rootstock) and is herbaceous in cold climates. In cool areas its self-seeding habit may be thought a nuisance but it is easy enough to cut off spent flowers to prevent seeding.

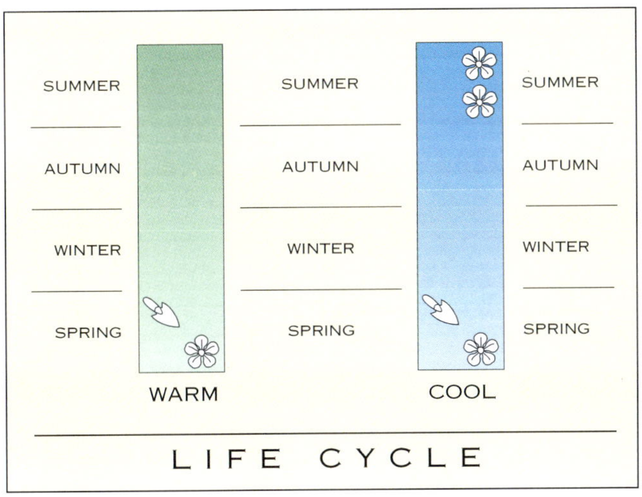

CONDITIONS

Climate Grows best in a cool climate but is worth trying in warm zones.

Aspect Grow this plant in full sun in cool areas and partial shade in warmer areas.

Soil Needs very well-drained soil enriched with decayed organic matter. Very acid soils should be limed by adding 100 g of lime or dolomite per square metre.

GROWING METHOD

Propagation Grows easily from ripe seed sown in autumn or from division of clumps in early spring.

Watering Water regularly during dry spring and summer weather but keep the soil rather dry during winter.

Fertilising Apply complete plant food when growth begins in spring.

Problems No specific pest or disease problems are known to attack this plant.

FLOWERING

Season The pretty blue flowers appear on numbers of stems, beginning in late spring and continuing throughout the summer months.

Cutting Flowers do not cut well.

AFTER FLOWERING

Requirements Cut off spent flowers as soon as they have faded if you do not want the seed to spread. Otherwise, leave the flowers until seed has set and ripened.

Japanese Windflower

Anemone* x *hybrida*, syn. *A. hupehensis* var. *japonica

ELEGANT SIMPLICITY is one way to describe the form of the Japanese windflower with its white, yellow and green colour scheme.

RELIABLE IN BLOOM year after year, the Japanese windflower is a useful and very attractive addition to the garden.

FEATURES

Also known as Japanese anemone, this herbaceous perennial is one of the great joys of the autumn garden. The leaves are three lobed, somewhat maple-like, and the single or double flowers are carried on stems up to 1 m high. Flowers may be single or double and may be white, or pale or deep pink. Once established, they spread into large clumps quite rapidly, travelling by underground stems and also self-seeding. Some gardeners consider them too invasive but unwanted plants can be dug out with little effort and a mass planting in full bloom is a real delight. These are best grown where they can remain undisturbed for some years. They are easy to grow and are ideally sited at the back of a shady garden bed or in dappled sunlight under trees.

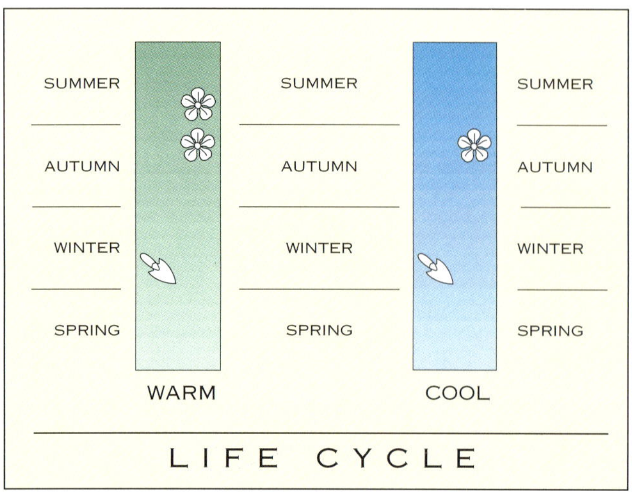

CONDITIONS

Climate Grows in cool, moist climates as well as in warm zones.

Aspect Prefers shade or semi-shade with shelter from strong wind.

Soil Grows best in well-drained soil that contains plenty of organic matter.

GROWING METHOD

Propagation Divide established clumps in late winter, ensuring that each division has some roots. For such a vigorous plant it can sometimes be tricky to divide and transplant. Replant the younger growths from the outside of the clump, about 30 cm apart.

Watering Needs regular watering in dry weather during the growing season.

Fertilising Fertilising is not essential but any complete plant food can be applied as new growth starts in spring.

Problems No specific problems are known.

FLOWERING

Season Flowers appear from late summer through the autumn months, depending on the weather and district.

Cutting Flowers are not suitable for cutting.

AFTER FLOWERING

Requirements Cut back flowered stems to ground level once they fade. The whole plant is then cut to the ground as foliage dies off.

KANGAROO PAW

Anigozanthos species and hybrids

THE STRANGE FORM of the flower is shown by this Anigozanthos manglesii.

KANGAROO PAWS will attract honey-eating birds, which take nectar from the flower tubes. The new hybrids are easier to grow as they are more resistant to disease than the original species.

FEATURES

One of Western Australia's most unusual looking plants, kangaroo paws vary in height from 30 cm to almost 2 m. The strap-like leaves form a clump and the strange looking woolly flowers are mainly in shades of red, green, yellow and orange. Flowers are long lasting and are widely used in the floral trade. Commonly grown species include *A. bicolor*, *A. flavidus*, *A. manglesii* and *A. viridis*. The hybrid plants sold under the name of 'Bush Gems' flower abundantly and appear to be resistant to ink disease, which affects most species. Plants grown in the right conditions last for many years. Kangaroo paws look their best planted in bold groups. They are mostly evergreen.

CONDITIONS

Climate Most prefer cool, wet winters and hot, dry summers. They dislike high summer humidity.

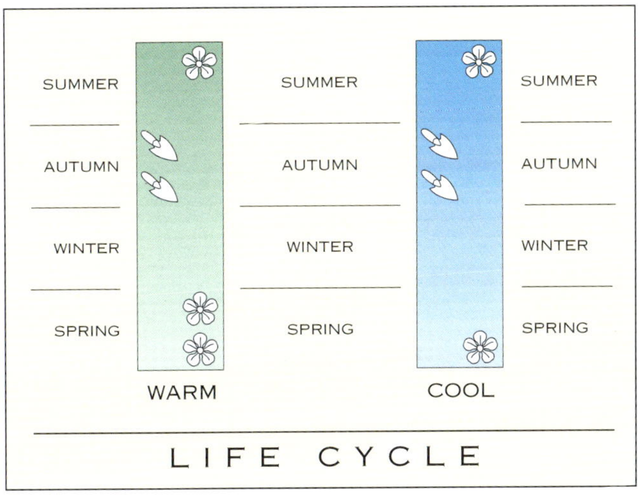

Aspect Most of these plants are best grown in an open, sunny position but some accept partial shade.

Soil Needs well-drained soil with an open, sandy or gravelly texture. If drainage is suspect, grow these plants in raised beds.

GROWING METHOD

Propagation Species can be grown from seed sown in autumn (plants may take three years to reach flowering size) or by dividing clumps in autumn. Hybrids must be divided. If dividing, reduce foliage by half to reduce moisture loss. Tissue culture, a laboratory procedure, is the only sure way to avoid disease. Space plants 25–70 cm apart, depending on variety.

Watering Water during active growth and give an occasional deep soaking in very dry conditions. Avoid overhead watering as this increases disease problems.

Fertilising Apply slow release fertiliser in autumn and again in spring with hybrids.

Problems Ink disease, a fungal problem, can be a serious problem for most species although the newer hybrids have much more resistance. Water plants around the roots only and spray with a fungicide if necessary.

FLOWERING

Season All flower at some time during spring and summer. The flowering display is long lasting.

Cutting The flowers cut well. Cut flowers close to the stem base.

AFTER FLOWERING

Requirements No pruning is needed beyond removal of spent flower stems. Remove any dead foliage, especially from the centre of the plant.

Kingfisher Daisy

Felicia amelloides

THE KINGFISHER BLUE flowers of this daisy are not done justice in photographs.

A LOW HEDGE of kingfisher daisy plants makes a pretty and unusual path edging. Regular dead-heading will keep the hedge in shape and prolong the flowering display.

FEATURES

This little evergreen daisy is a great standby in the garden as it is in flower for many months of the year, especially if it is regularly dead-headed. It can grow to around 50 cm high but is often much shorter, although it can spread about 30 cm wide. It has neat, rounded leaves and the small daisy flowers are bright sky-blue. Sometimes cultivars with larger flowers are found and there is a variety with white and green variegated leaves. Kingfisher daisy can be planted towards the front of a garden bed with mixed annuals and perennials or in a sunny rock garden. It can also be grown in containers, giving good decorative value in balcony and patio gardens.

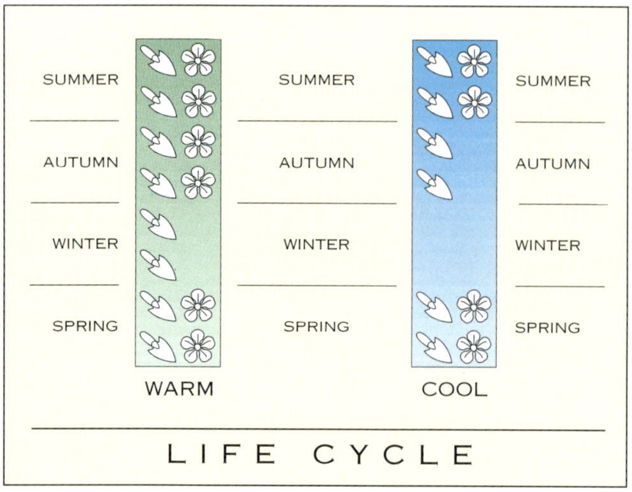

CONDITIONS

Climate Grows best in a warm to hot climate but can be grown in cool climates if frost is not severe.

Aspect Prefers full sun all day.

Soil Must have well-drained soil. Soils enriched with organic matter will produce better plants.

GROWING METHOD

Propagation Grows easily from cuttings taken from spring to autumn and can also be grown from seed sown in late summer or autumn. Take fresh cuttings about every three years to maintain compact plants. Plant 20–25 cm apart.

Watering Although tolerant of some dryness once established, it does respond to regular watering in the warmer months.

Fertilising Apply complete plant food in spring and again in early summer.

Problems No specific problems are known.

FLOWERING

Season Has a long flowering through spring into summer, with fewer blooms in autumn.

Cutting Flowers can be cut for the vase but stems are short—use it in a mini posy.

AFTER FLOWERING

Requirements Regularly remove spent flowers to prolong the blooming period. Bushes that are sprawling can be cut back fairly hard in late winter.

LADY'S MANTLE

Alchemilla mollis

LONG USED as a folk medicine to help heal wounds and gynaecological problems, lady's mantle is today usually grown for its decorative value. The pure lime-green flowers can light up the garden and they are shown to advantage against the heavy-textured, lobed leaves.

FEATURES

This is a quick-growing herbaceous perennial mostly used as a border plant along the edges of paths and garden beds. It is good for suppressing weeds and sows itself freely, often popping up in cracks in paths or paving. Growing anywhere between 20 and 40 cm high, one plant may spread to 30 or 40 cm. The rounded, slightly hairy leaves overlap one another and the plant produces trusses of bright lime-green flowers through summer. It provides a lovely contrast with other, stronger colours. Even out of flower the foliage looks pretty and the leaves tend to trap raindrops or dew, thus greatly adding to the decorative effect of this plant.

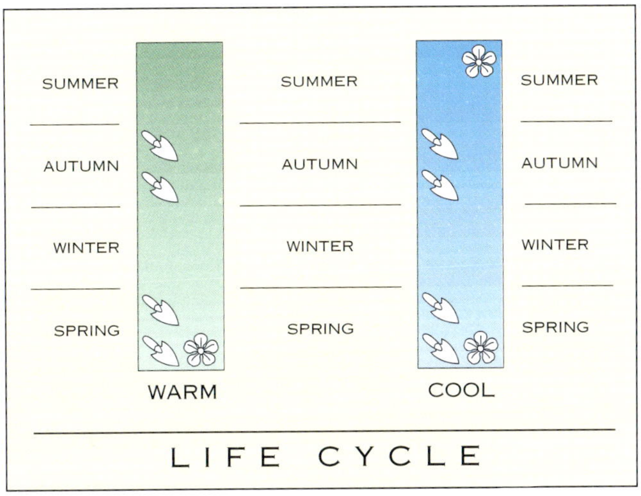

CONDITIONS

Climate Grows best in cool to cold areas but it can be grown in warm zones if it is not too humid.

Aspect Tolerates full sun in cold climates but needs partial shade elsewhere.

Soil Needs well-drained soil that has a high organic content.

GROWING METHOD

Propagation Self-sown seedlings can be easily transplanted to other positions. Clumps can be divided in either autumn or spring, with divisions spaced 20–25 cm apart.

Watering Needs ample water throughout spring and summer for its best appearance but it tolerates dry periods.

Fertilising Apply blood and bone or complete plant food as new growth begins.

Problems No specific problems are known.

FLOWERING

Season Masses of lime-green flowers appear from late spring through summer.

Cutting Flowers do not cut well.

AFTER FLOWERING

Requirements If you don't want plants to self-seed, remove spent flowers as they fade. Once flowering has finished and growth begins to die down the plants can be cut back hard.

LAMB'S EARS

Stachys byzantina, syn. *S. lanata*

LAMB'S EARS needs good drainage and so growing it in a container may be the ideal solution if your soil is too heavy.

MORE TRADITIONAL is this planting, where lamb's ears edge a garden bed. The plants will multiply rapidly if they like the situation.

FEATURES

Lamb's ears is a low-growing, evergreen perennial most often used as an edging plant. It could also be used in pockets of a rock garden, but wherever it is planted it must have excellent drainage and full exposure to sun. The leaves are densely covered with hairs, giving them a white or pale grey, woolly appearance which accounts for its common name. It does produce pinky purple flowers on spikes that stand up above the foliage but these are not especially attractive—it is grown for its foliage, not its flowers. A cultivar, 'Sheila McQueen', has very woolly flowers useful in dried flower arrangements if they are cut as soon as they are fully open. Plants grow only 15–20 cm high but can spread a good distance. The low-growing form 'Silver Carpet' may grow only 10–15 cm high.

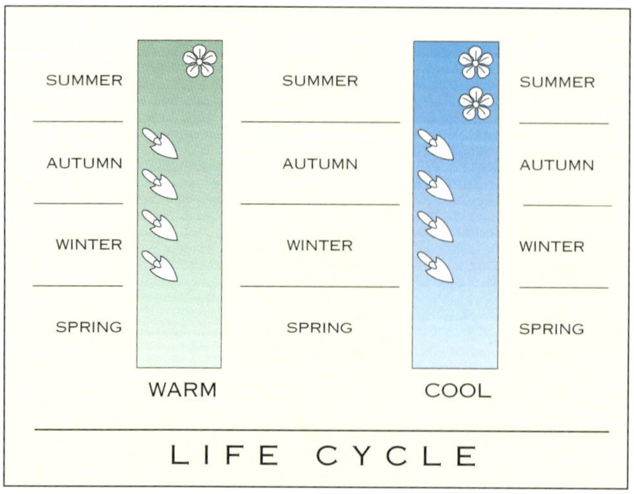

CONDITIONS

Climate Prefers a cool climate but can be grown in warm regions if humidity is not high.

Aspect Must be in full sun all day for best results.

Soil Needs very fast draining soil. It grows well in poor, sandy or gravelly soil.

GROWING METHOD

Propagation Grows readily from cuttings that are taken in late summer to early autumn. Established clumps can also be divided during winter, with the new divisions being planted out about 20 cm apart.

Watering Water regularly to establish. Once plants are established, water only very occasionally.

Fertilising Grows without supplementary fertiliser but you could apply a little complete plant food in early spring.

Problems There are no specific problems but plants will fail if overwatered, if drainage is poor or if the climate is warm and very humid.

FLOWERING

Season Flowers are produced in summer, sometimes into autumn.

Cutting Lamb's ears are not good as a vase flower but they can be cut and dried for later use.

AFTER FLOWERING

Requirements Cut out spent flower stems right at the base. Trailing growth can be shortened back at any time but plants may need to be cut back hard in late winter.

LEWISIA

Lewisia species and hybrids

GARDENERS in cool climates can enjoy the beauty of lewisia, as long as they can provide the rather demanding growing requirements.

GRAVEL PROVIDES perfect drainage for this lovely pink lewisia, which here grows in company with a pink aubrieta.

FEATURES

Lewisias are very low-growing, compact perennials. They are succulent plants that form tight, flat rosettes of foliage with their colourful flowers standing 15–20 cm above the foliage. The rosettes on some can eventually grow 15–20 cm wide. Although some species are deciduous, those most commonly grown are evergreen, being cultivars of *L. cotyledon* and *L. columbiana*. Deciduous species tend to be grown by specialists. Some varieties have striped flowers while others come in straight colours of white, cream, yellow, apricot, pink and red. These plants are very specific in their requirements and must generally be grown in rock gardens or in crevices in drystone walls. They may be grown in a very coarse medium in pots with a layer of coarse sand or crushed sandstone as mulch. With the right growing conditions this makes a delightful plant.

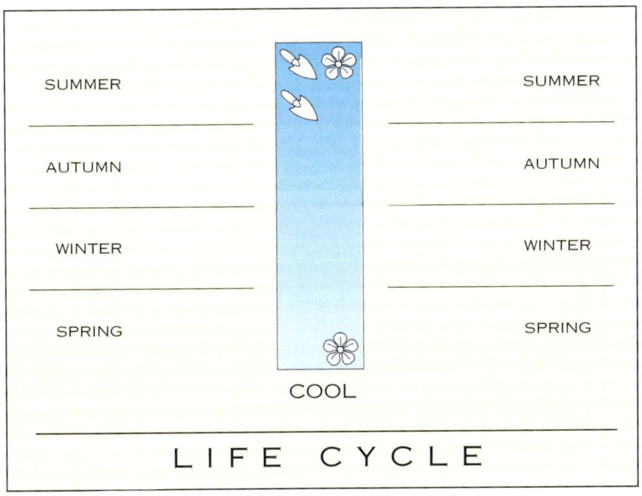

CONDITIONS

Climate This is a plant that can be grown only in cool or cold climates.

Aspect Preferred aspect varies from full sun in very cold climates to partial shade in cool areas.

Soil Needs perfect drainage such as very coarse, gravelly soil or it can be planted in pockets of a drystone wall.

GROWING METHOD

Propagation Dark, glossy seeds that appear after the flowers have fallen can be collected in late summer and autumn, stored in the refrigerator (not the freezer) and sown in spring. It also grows from offsets taken from the parent plant in summer. Plant about 15–20 cm apart.

Watering Water in dry weather in spring and summer, allowing it to dry out between waterings. Keep it drier in autumn and as dry as possible during the winter months.

Fertilising Apply a little blood and bone in early spring.

Problems There are few problems except those that result from poor growing conditions such as poor drainage and overwatering.

FLOWERING

Season Flowers appear in spring and early summer.

Cutting Flowers are unsuitable for cutting.

AFTER FLOWERING

Requirements Remove spent flowers unless you are waiting for seed to ripen. Pot-grown plants can be repotted after flowering. Remove dead leaves from plants at any time.

LIRIOPE

Liriope muscari

FLOWER SPIKES in deep violet add to the attraction of liriope, which is usually grown for its foliage. This is a variegated form.

AMONG ITS many uses, liriope makes an excellent edging for garden beds. Here it accentuates the circular form of the fountain.

FEATURES

This plant, also known as lilyturf, is sometimes confused with *Ophiopogon jaburan*, also called lilyturf and a close relative of mondo grass. The two are very similar but the *Ophiopogon* has white flowers. Liriope grows about 30–35 cm high. The species has dark green leaves but there are variegated forms also. A spike of deep violet flowers stands well above the leaves. This decorative foliage plant is herbaceous, dying back almost to the ground even in fairly mild areas, but it is a tough and useful plant for the garden.

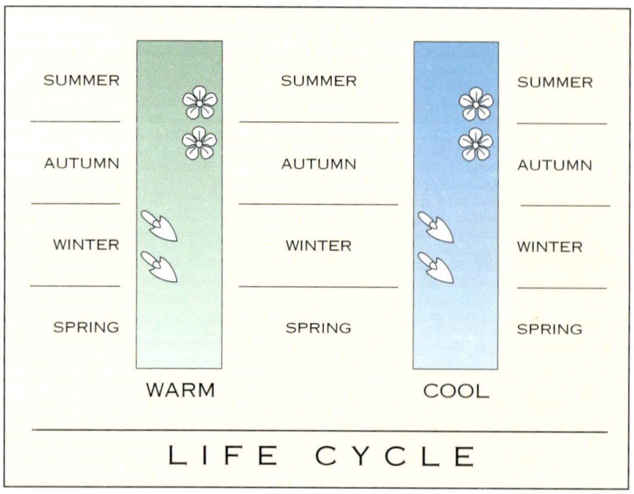

CONDITIONS

Climate Grows in cool or warm areas but will not do well in the tropics.

Aspect Prefers shade or dappled sunlight, or full sun for only part of the day.

Soil Tolerates most soils but does best in well-drained soil enriched with organic matter.

GROWING METHOD

Propagation The easiest method of increase is to lift and divide clumps in winter. Replant divisions 8–10 cm apart.

Watering Water regularly during dry spring and summer weather. Plants tolerate drought but prefer some regular water.

Fertilising Apply complete plant food in spring.

Problems No specific problems are known.

FLOWERING

Season The flowers appear in late summer to early autumn and last well on the plant.

Cutting Flowers do not pick well.

AFTER FLOWERING

Requirements Cut off spent flower heads once flowers have dropped. As growth dies down towards winter, cut it off cleanly.

LOBELIA

Lobelia cardinalis

THIS LOBELIA is also known as cardinal flower, an apt description as the tall spikes of flowers are the same scarlet as a cardinal's robes.

IN ITS NATURAL HABITAT in North America this lobelia grows on wet meadows and river banks. It needs lots of moisture.

FEATURES

Lobelia to most people is a small edging plant with bright blue flowers. There are, however, about 400 species of lobelia, many of them perennials. This herbaceous species with bright scarlet flowers is also known as cardinal flower and grows to about 1 m in height. With its dark green leaves and bright flowers it really stands out and it is sometimes used as a feature plant. It can also be used in a mixed border or mass planted among shrubs as long as the ground retains plenty of moisture. Pink or white forms are seen but it is the bright red that is most popular. It establishes readily.

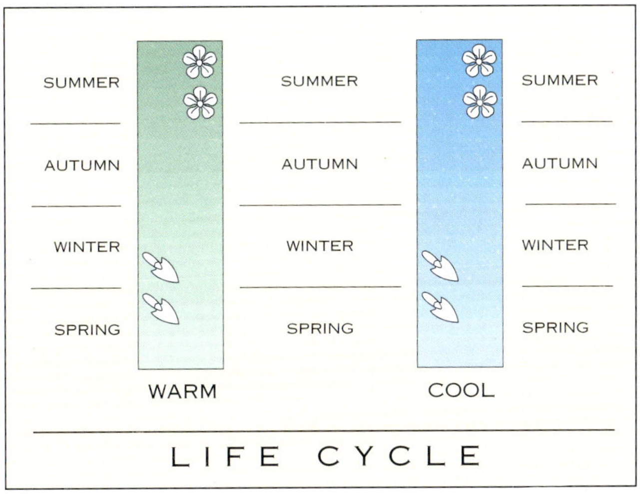

CONDITIONS

Climate Grows best in cool areas but is worth trying in warm zones.

Aspect Grows in full sun or semi-shade.

Soil Needs rich and moisture-retentive soil as these plants are not tolerant of drought.

GROWING METHOD

Propagation Plants are usually divided every two or three years in late winter or early spring. Plant divisions about 30 cm apart.

Watering Lobelia must be kept moist and well watered while it is in active growth throughout spring and summer.

Fertilising Apply complete plant food and a mulch of compost or manure as soon as growth begins during spring.

Problems No specific pest or disease problems are known to attack this plant.

FLOWERING

Season There is a long flowering period through the summer months.

Cutting Flowers are not suitable for cutting.

AFTER FLOWERING

Requirements Cut off spent flower stems. Tidy up foliage as it dies down.

Lungwort

Pulmonaria

EARLY FLOWERING makes lungwort a favourite plant for cool climate gardens.

THE SPOTTED FOLIAGE of lungwort makes a dense and attractive groundcover under trees. It is a reliable grower as long as it gets regular water in spring and summer.

FEATURES

Lungwort is a plant well suited to planting under trees, between shrubs or at the front of a shady border. The flowers appear well before the foliage and are mostly in shades of blue, although some flowers open pink and change to blue. The abundance of flowers makes this well worth growing in cool areas. The foliage is very handsome, often silver spotted, and the whole plant is rarely more than 25–30 cm high. When formed into a spreading mat 30 cm or more wide, it is very decorative even out of flower. Both the botanical and common names refer to lungs: it was once believed each plant resembled the part of the body that could be treated with it.

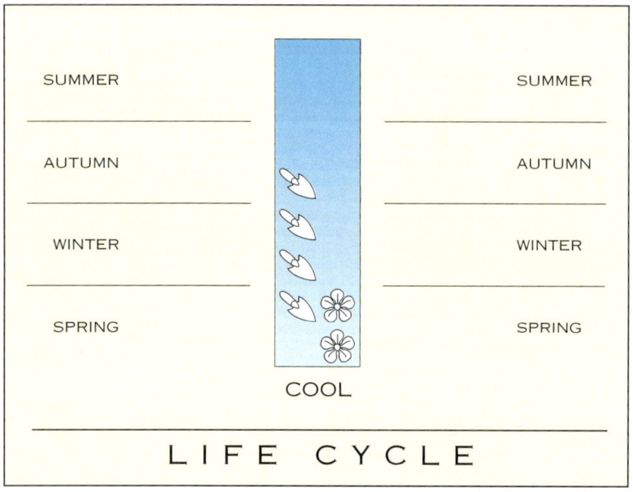

CONDITIONS

Climate Suitable for cool climates only.

Aspect Grows best in light shade under trees or in borders that are shady during the hottest part of the day.

Soil The soil should be heavily enriched with decayed organic matter but it should drain quite well.

GROWING METHOD

Propagation Grows from seed or division of clumps from late autumn to very early spring. Replant divisions about 15 cm apart.

Watering Needs constant soil moisture during the growing season.

Fertilising Apply a little complete fertiliser in early spring and mulch well.

Problems No specific problems are known.

FLOWERING

Season Most lungworts flower early in the spring.

Cutting Flowers do not cut well.

AFTER FLOWERING

Requirements Spent flowers can be cut off if you do not want seeding to occur. Flowers are finished in spring but the foliage stays looking fresh over many months, and so little attention is needed until autumn when the foliage can be tidied up as it begins to die off.

LUPIN

Lupinus polyphyllus hybrids

RUSSELL LUPINS are noteworthy for their rich colours, including this pinky-red.

LUPINS ARE traditional favourites for cool climate perennial borders, where they provide vertical interest. They grow here among oriental poppies, campion and grey-leaved germander.

FEATURES

This herbaceous perennial lupin is generally known as the Russell lupin, named after the hybridiser who began developing many fine strains of these plants early this century. It produces tall, densely packed spires of blooms in a myriad of colours and the foliage is attractive too. Growing well over 1 m high, these are plants for massed display or for the back of a perennial border. Although they can be cut for indoor use they give more value in the garden. Russell lupin is best grown in cool climates where plants may produce several spikes per plant whereas in warmer areas only one spike may appear and plants may not survive as perennials. Plants can be short lived and should be divided regularly to maintain vigorous growth.

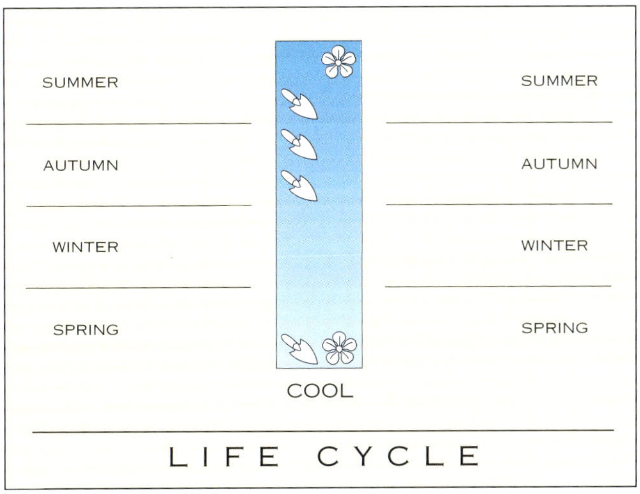

CONDITIONS

Climate Prefers a cool area; not suitable for warm areas.

Aspect Grows in full sun or semi-shade but needs wind protection.

Soil Soil need not be rich but must be well drained.

GROWING METHOD

Propagation Division of these plants may be difficult. Many strains come true from seed, which should be soaked in warm water before planting in late summer to autumn. Cuttings can be taken from new shoots emerging from the crown in early spring. Set plants out 30–40 cm apart.

Watering Give ample water through spring and summer.

Fertilising Needs little fertiliser as lupins fix nitrogen in nodules on their roots. Low nitrogen fertiliser may be applied as buds begin to form.

Problems Powdery mildew may be a problem in humid conditions; if necessary spray with a fungicide registered for this disease. Crowns may rot if plants are set too deep or if drainage is poor.

FLOWERING

Season There is a long flowering period through late spring and early summer.

Cutting Flowers may be cut for the vase.

AFTER FLOWERING

Requirements Cut off spent flower stems as soon as blooms have faded—you may get a second flush. When plants die down in late autumn or winter, cut them off at ground level.

MARGUERITE DAISY

Argyranthemum frutescens

EASY-TO-GROW MARGUERITES will provide a cheerful patch of colour in the garden as long as they are dead-headed regularly.

MASSES OF marguerite daisies in peak condition can make just as splendid a show of sweeping colour as more demanding plants.

FEATURES

Daisy bushes are great value in any garden, making a mounded evergreen shrub about 1 m high and wide. They are an essential feature of cottage gardens but fit in with most garden styles. They can be grown in containers, too, and so are useful for balcony and courtyard gardens. With regular dead-heading they can be in bloom for many months and the flowers are very good for cutting. Originally only in white or yellow, there are now several pink forms available. All colours come in singles or doubles. Marguerite daisies are vigorous growers and fairly short lived but they strike so easily from cuttings that you need never be without them. Plants start to look woody after a few years. Strike cuttings and when they've taken, dig out the old plant.

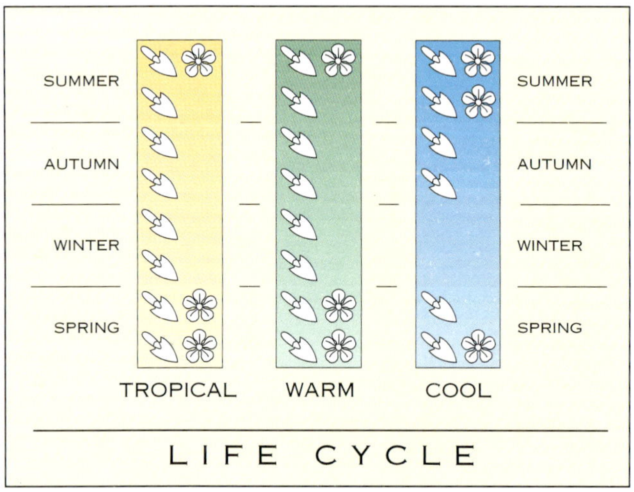

CONDITIONS

Climate Grows well from the tropics to cool regions.
Aspect Prefers full sun all day.
Soil Grows in a wide range of soils but they must be well drained.

GROWING METHOD

Propagation Grows easily from soft-tip or firm cuttings taken almost any time of year. Cuttings generally root within 3–4 weeks. Space plants around 1 m apart.
Watering Needs regular watering to establish. For best growth and blooming deep watering is needed every week or two during dry, warm weather.
Fertilising Apply complete plant food in late winter. Supplementary feeding is not necessary for daisies but an occasional application of fertiliser may give larger blooms.
Problems Leafminers occasionally damage foliage. Cut off damaged leaves or cut back the whole plant hard to get rid of the pest.

FLOWERING

Season There is a long flowering period through spring and summer if spent flowers are regularly removed.
Cutting Cutting flowers will extend blooming. Change the water frequently to prolong vase life.

AFTER FLOWERING

Requirements To maintain their shape, cut bushes back by about half in autumn.

MATILIJA POPPY

Romneya coulteri

CRIMPED WHITE PETALS surround a large mass of golden stamens to make the beautiful matilija poppy flower.

THE BLUE-GREEN FOLIAGE and splendid white flowers of matilija poppy make an eye-catching contribution to the garden.

FEATURES

Also known as Californian tree poppy, this lovely perennial is not always easy to accommodate. It is native to the canyons and dry riverbeds in parts of California, where there is generally rain only in winter and where summers are hot and dry. When conditions are suitable this plant can spread with underground roots to produce suckers. The large white flowers that appear in spring and summer have beautiful crinkled petals that look like silk. Plants grow from 1 m to over 2 m high and the blue-green foliage is deeply cut and very attractive. Place these perennials in groups among shrubs or with other mixed perennials. Most plants available are likely to be hybrids of the straight species and *R. coulteri* var. *trichocalyx.*

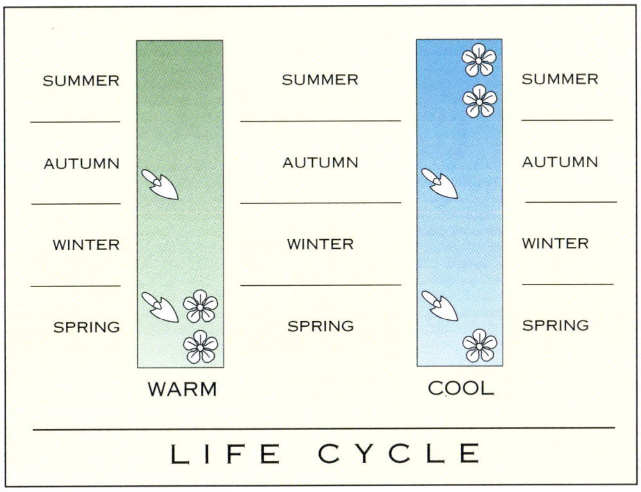

CONDITIONS

Climate Grows in cool or warm areas. The high humidity and summer rain of many tropical areas would probably kill these plants.

Aspect Needs full sun all day.

Soil Needs very well-drained, preferably sandy or gravelly loam. It cannot be grown in clay soils.

GROWING METHOD

Propagation Grows from seed sown in autumn but is easiest propagated from root cuttings or suckers growing away from the main plant in spring. Wait until plants are very well established before attempting to disturb the roots. Space plants around 40 cm apart.

Watering Water regularly in spring when the foliage is growing and buds are appearing; thereafter water only occasionally in very dry weather.

Fertilising Give a little complete plant food in early spring.

Problems Poor drainage and overwatering can kill matilija poppies.

FLOWERING

Season Depending on the area, plants will flower from mid-spring through summer.

Cutting Like all poppies these make lovely cut flowers. Scald or burn the stems before arranging.

AFTER FLOWERING

Requirements Cut off spent flowers. As this plant flowers on new growth it is best to cut it down to the ground in winter. Mulch well in cold zones.

Meadow Rue

Thalictrum aquilegifolium

THE FLUFFY PINK FLOWERS of meadow rue are not long lasting but the pretty foliage persists until autumn.

FINER FOLIAGE, smaller starry flowers and very full growth are features of the related Thalictrum delavayi *and its cultivars.*

FEATURES

Easy and quick to grow, this herbaceous perennial grows to around a metre high. The rather fern-like, blue-green foliage is attractively lobed, and the flowers are mauve-pink in dense, fluffy heads. While the floral display does not last a long time the foliage adds charm to the garden over many months. Meadow rue can be planted in mixed borders or in clumps in light shade under trees. There are a number of cultivars, including a white form and one with deeper violet blooms. Another meadow rue worth seeking out is *T. delavayi* (syn. *T. dipterocarpum*) and its cultivars 'Album' and 'Hewitt's Double'. This has finer foliage and the pink-mauve flowers are star shaped, with central hanging stamens.

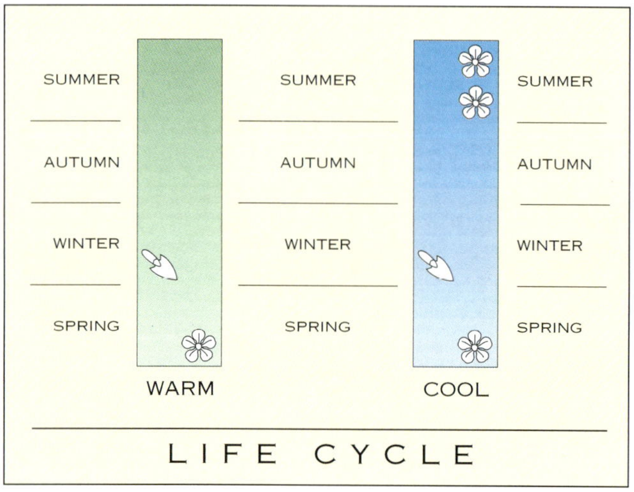

CONDITIONS

Climate Grows in cool and warm regions but not in tropical areas.

Aspect Prefers light shade or morning sun and afternoon shade. In cool districts it can be grown in full sun.

Soil Likes well-drained soil that has been enriched with organic matter.

GROWING METHOD

Propagation Grows from seed sown in autumn or divisions of a clump made in late winter. Plant divisions 25–30 cm apart.

Watering Likes regular, deep watering through spring and summer.

Fertilising As growth begins in spring apply complete plant food and mulch around plants with well-decayed manure or compost.

Problems No specific pest or disease problems are known for this plant.

FLOWERING

Season Flowers appear some time during late spring and summer, depending on climate.

Cutting Flowers do not cut well.

AFTER FLOWERING

Requirements Cut off any spent flower stems unless you want to save seed. When plants die down in late autumn, cut off the foliage to just above ground level.

MECONOPSIS

Meconopsis betonicifolia

NO OTHER blue flower has quite the same startlingly clear colour as the amazing blue poppy, a true delight whenever it can be grown.

WOODLAND CONDITIONS where the soil never really dries out are essential for this plant. It flowers well in this garden every year.

FEATURES

Meconopsis is the beautiful blue poppy everyone would love to grow. There is probably no other plant that produces such an intense sky-blue flower. It is, however, not easy to grow as it demands a cool to cold climate and woodland conditions. Its natural habitat is very high altitude alpine meadows in China. Plants do not flower the first year and they die down in winter, growing and blooming the second year. It is said that if meconopsis is prevented from blooming the first time it sets buds, it is more likely to become perennial. Meconopsis can be short lived, even in cold climates. Growing to almost 2 m in its habitat, in cultivation it is more likely to be 50–70 cm high.

LIFE CYCLE

CONDITIONS

Climate A cool to cold, moist climate is essential.

Aspect Needs partial shade; protect from strong wind.

Soil Needs a well-drained soil that is rich in organic matter.

GROWING METHOD

Propagation Grows from fresh seed sown in autumn. Keep seedlings fairly dry through winter and plant them out in early spring. Dormant roots may be moved in winter and planted 25 cm apart.

Watering Needs an ample supply of water through spring and summer but should never be waterlogged or crowns will rot.

Fertilising Apply a little blood and bone as growth begins in spring.

Problems Overwet soil, especially during winter, will rot the crown. Downy mildew may be a problem in some seasons. If so, spray plants with an appropriate fungicide.

FLOWERING

Season Flowers may appear from late spring throughout summer.

Cutting Blooms may be cut but they will last longer on the plant.

AFTER FLOWERING

Requirements Remove spent flower stems unless you are waiting for seed to ripen. Once growth dies down, cut it off at ground level.

MILFOIL
Achillea millefolium

LONG FLOWERING and not as invasive as the species, the new hybrid milfoils will give pleasure for months.

MILFOIL is also known as yarrow, soldier's woundwort, nosebleed and sanguinary, the last three reflecting its use in herbal medicine.

FEATURES

Milfoil or yarrow is a vigorous perennial growing from 50 cm to over 1 m high. The species has flattish heads of white flowers and feathery foliage but cultivars have flowers in a lovely range of shades, including yellow, pink, apricot and crimson. Flowers are long lasting. Milfoil is quick and easy to establish and may need to be controlled if it exceeds its allotted space. It has become weedy in some parts of the world but runners are easy to pull out. Some of the cultivars are less invasive than the species. *A. filipendulina*, fern-leaf yarrow, has flat heads of bright yellow flowers that last all summer. Selected forms have deep or pale yellow blooms. Best planted in large drifts, these plants are ideal for the back of borders or as permanent plantings among annuals.

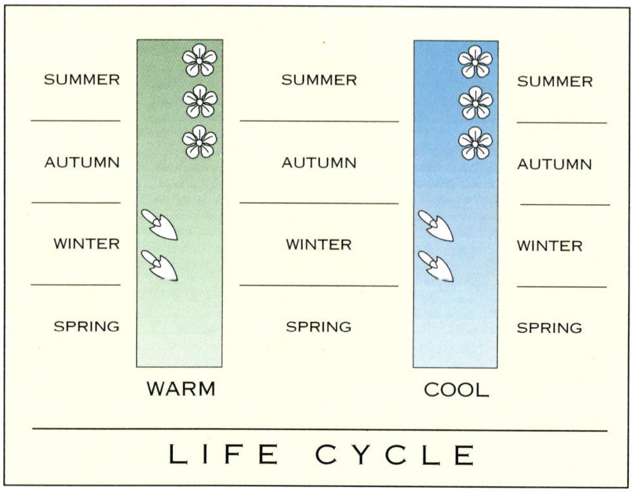

CONDITIONS

Climate Grows well in almost any climate except in tropical regions.

Aspect Needs full sun for best results but tolerates shade for part of the day.

Soil Any well-drained soil is suitable.

GROWING METHOD

Propagation Grows easily if established clumps are lifted and divided in winter. Plant the divisions 20–30 cm apart.

Watering Needs regular watering to establish new spring growth but once established milfoil is drought tolerant and needs only occasional deep watering.

Fertilising Apply complete plant food as growth commences in spring.

Problems No specific pest or disease problems are known to attack milfoil.

FLOWERING

Season The long flowering period lasts throughout summer into early autumn. Regular removal of the spent flower stems will prolong blooming.

Cutting Flowers are good for cutting as they have a reasonably long vase life. Cut flowers for the vase as soon as the heads are fully open.

AFTER FLOWERING

Requirements Cut off any spent flower stalks that remain on the bush. In winter cut off all foliage just above the ground.

MISCANTHUS

Miscanthus sinensis

FINE STRIPES in cream and green make 'Variegatus' a popular form of miscanthus.

ZEBRA GRASS is the common name given to 'Zebrinus', with its yellow-spotted horizontal markings. Ornamental grasses can provide useful contrast in the perennial garden.

FEATURES

This is a group of large, ornamental, herbaceous perennial grasses. The plain green species is not often grown as the many cultivars with striped or banded foliage are much more decorative. Cultivars range in height from about 80 cm to 2 m although many grow about 1.2 m high. Clumps spread from short, thick rhizomes and will become very wide after a few years if not divided. Commonly grown cultivars include 'Zebrinus' with distinct horizontal gold banding and 'Variegatus' with long cream or white stripes, while other varieties such as 'Silver Feather', 'Morning Light' and 'Purpurascens' are worth seeking out. All produce pale creamy beige feathery plumes of flowers in autumn and good autumn colour is produced from the foliage of some varieties in cold climates. Miscanthus can be grown at the back of a border or as a feature plant and it looks well planted beside a pond.

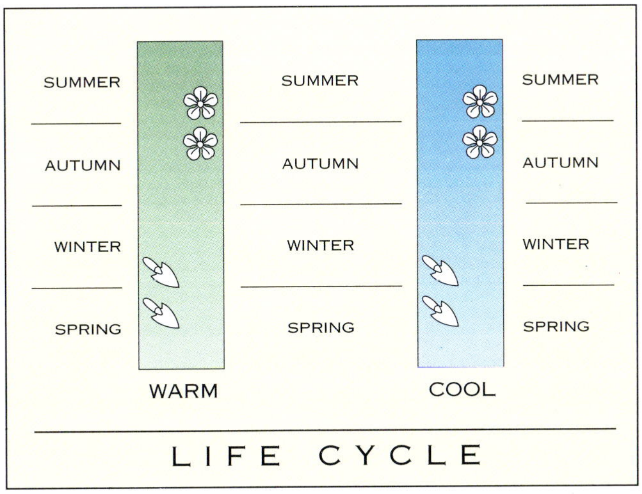

CONDITIONS

Climate Grows quite successfully in both cool and warm climates.

Aspect Grows best in full sun but tolerates shade for part of the day.

Soil Prefers a soil heavily enriched with organic matter to aid in moisture retention.

GROWING METHOD

Propagation Clumps can be lifted and divided in late winter or early spring. This can require considerable effort as roots are very tenacious. Replant divisions about 30 cm apart, or closer if you want quicker coverage.

Watering These grasses need regular watering during spring and summer to look their best.

Fertilising Complete plant food can be applied in spring but is not essential if the soil contains plenty of manure or compost.

Problems No specific pest or disease problems are known for this plant.

FLOWERING

Season Flowering plumes appear well above the foliage in autumn.

Cutting Plumes do not last well when cut. They last better in the garden.

AFTER FLOWERING

Requirements Unless you are in a very cold climate it is probably best to cut off plumes before the seed disperses as the weed potential of these plants is not well documented. Once foliage starts to die off and become unsightly, cut it off at ground level.

MULLEIN

Verbascum

SEVERAL CULTIVARS of mullein are in these pale coppery tones, which combine well with other pastel shades in the garden.

MULLEINS HAVE few equals as accent plants as they are tough and adaptable, capable of tolerating many climates and conditions.

FEATURES

Not all mulleins are reliably perennial, some being best treated as biennials and replaced after two years. However, most are easy to raise. They are grown for their large rosettes of foliage, often silver or grey, from which emerges a tall spike of flowers sometimes well over 1 m high. They make striking accent plants in any sunny part of the garden. The various species and their cultivars have flowers in a range of colours, including white and shades of yellow, pink and purple. The common mullein, *V. thapsus*, also known as Aaron's rod, has become naturalised and weedy in some parts of the world—consider this before planting it. Mullein has a long history of use by humans, first as a candle and then in folk medicine.

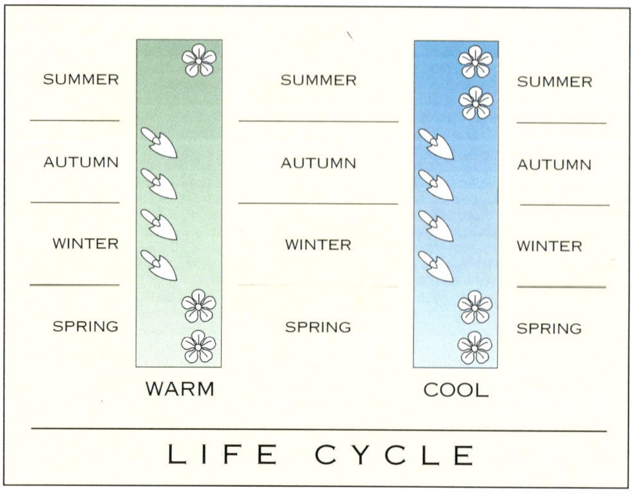

CONDITIONS

Climate Most species come from dry habitats and so are ideal for areas of low rainfall. Most can be grown in cool and warm areas, as well as in the dry tropics.

Aspect Grows best in full sun all day.

Soil Grows in any kind of well-drained soil.

GROWING METHOD

Propagation Grows from seed sown as soon as it is ripe or from root cuttings taken in autumn or winter. Seed forms on the spike after the flowers have fallen and it will be ripe when it has changed colour to a brown or black. Plants of most mullein species need to be planted out about 1 m apart.

Watering Give regular watering in early spring as new growth begins. Once established, plants can tolerate drought.

Fertilising Apply complete plant food in early spring.

Problems No specific problems are known.

FLOWERING

Season Mulleins flower in spring through to summer, depending on species and district.

Cutting As the flower spike opens very gradually this is not a good cut flower but it is a striking garden feature.

AFTER FLOWERING

Requirements Cut off the spent flower spike unless you want seed to set.

OBEDIENT PLANT

Physostegia virginiana

THE SHORT SPIKES of flowers are attached to the obedient plant by a joint so that they can be rearranged as you please.

OBEDIENT PLANT looks best in large plantings and it's well worth devoting garden space to it as the flowers last for several months.

FEATURES

Obedient plant is an easy-care, fast-growing perennial suitable for a wide range of climates. It spreads by stolons (runners) and also by seed so that large clumps can develop in one season. Excess plants are not too difficult to remove. The dark green leaves are only 10–15 cm high but flowering stems may be from 40 to 80 cm tall. The flowers in the species are pinky-mauve but there are cultivars with flowers in various shades of pink, red and white. This is a very good cut flower. It looks its best planted in large drifts in a border or among other garden shrubs. The common name refers to the fact that flowers remain fixed the way they are turned. It is also known as false dragon's head in some areas.

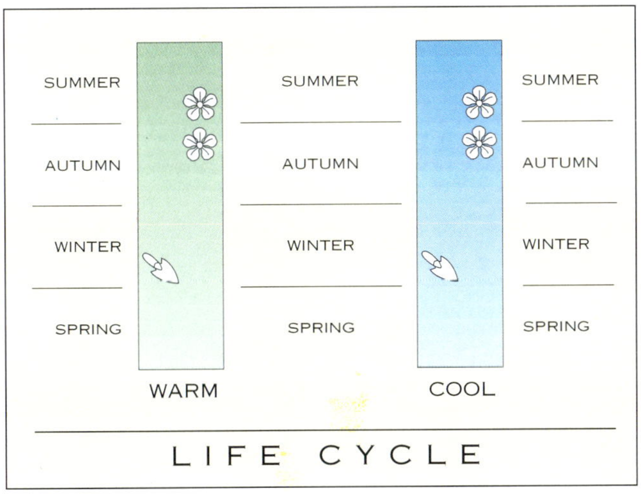

CONDITIONS

Climate Grows in all zones except the tropics.

Aspect Grows in full sun or semi-shade. Some protection from strong wind is desirable.

Soil Tolerates a range of soils but best results come with well-drained soil rich in organic matter.

GROWING METHOD

Propagation Divide old clumps in late winter, planting new divisions in groups for best effect. Plant single individuals about 10 cm apart. The oldest plants can be discarded. Because of its vigorous habit you need to divide every couple of years.

Watering Tolerates dry periods well although plants and blooms will be small in drought conditions. Looks best if given regular, deep watering in spring and summer.

Fertilising Apply complete plant food in spring. Mulch with decayed organic matter at the same time.

Problems No specific problems are known.

FLOWERING

Season Flowers can be produced from middle to late summer into autumn.

Cutting Frequent cutting of blooms should produce a second flush of flowers. Scald cut stems to prolong their vase life.

AFTER FLOWERING

Requirements Remove spent flower stems and tidy up growth as it dies down.

OYSTER PLANT

Acanthus mollis

LITTLE FLOWERS in purple and white open along tall spikes above the foliage.

ALTHOUGH THEY prefer shade, the oyster plants in this cool climate garden are growing very happily in the open. The masses of handsome foliage suit a large garden best.

FEATURES

Also known as 'bear's breeches', this handsome foliage plant grows from 70 cm to 1 m high and can make a clump close to 1 m wide. The dark glossy leaves provided the inspiration and model for the decoration on Corinthian columns and are depicted in many forms of art. This is a striking feature plant for a shady garden. It is at its best when mass planted if space allows but one generous clump can be effective in a small garden. The stiff flower spikes of purple and white flowers appear among the foliage during spring or summer. It can be quite a vigorous grower although it dies back after flowering. It can multiply rather quickly once established but is not troublesome. This plant is easy to care for as long as it is not short of water.

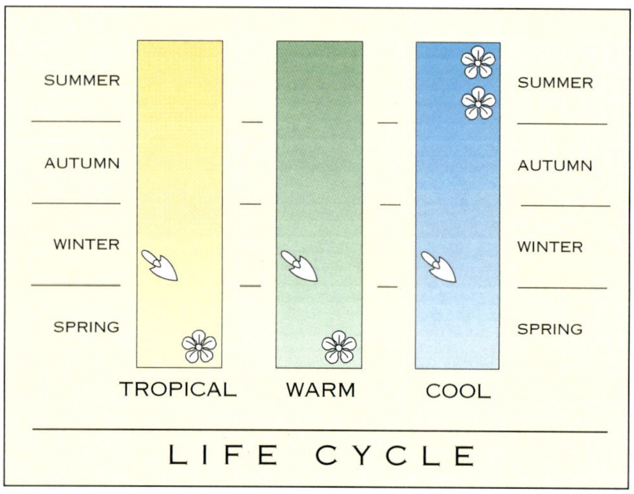

CONDITIONS

Climate Grows well from the tropics to cool areas.

Aspect Prefers shade or semi-shade but tolerates sun for part of the day.

Soil Needs well-drained soil that contains plenty of organic matter to aid in some water retention. Mulch plants with decayed manure or compost.

GROWING METHOD

Propagation Grows from seed sown in spring but is easiest to grow by dividing clumps in late winter. Plant new divisions 30–40 cm apart.

Watering Must be given ample water in dry weather during spring and summer. After flowering cut back on watering.

Fertilising Apply complete plant food as growth starts during spring.

Problems Slugs and snails can cause a lot of damage to young growth and so take precautions. No other problems are known.

FLOWERING

Season The tall spikes of purple and white flowers appear in late spring and summer.

Cutting It may be possible to use this as a cut flower but it will give better value in the garden.

AFTER FLOWERING

Requirements Cut off the flowering stem once it has faded. No other pruning is needed beyond removal of any dead leaves.

Pasque Flower

Pulsatilla vulgaris

FOLK MEDICINE makes use of the pasque flower but it should be treated with caution as it can be fatal if used incorrectly.

LIGHT FROST here coats buds of the pasque flower, showing up the silky hairs. They will be more obvious on the seed heads.

FEATURES

The soft purple flowers appear before the leaves on this small perennial, which is among the earliest flowers to bloom in spring. The whole plant is covered with silky hairs, giving it a delicate appearance that belies its hardy nature. After the flowers have fallen, a fluffy seed head is formed and these decorative heads persist for a long time. The finely divided leaves grow from 10 to 15 cm tall while the flowers may be on stems from 10 to 30 cm high. Pasque flower should be planted in groups or drifts to get the best effect. There are now pink, white and red forms available. Leaves and flowers of this plant may cause skin irritation, and so wear gloves when handling it if you have sensitive skin.

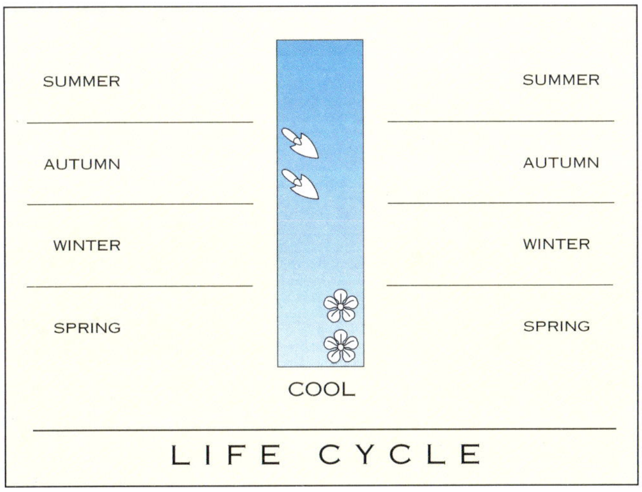

CONDITIONS

Climate Prefers a cool climate but will grow in some warm areas.

Aspect Prefers full sun but tolerates semi-shade, especially in warmer districts.

Soil Needs well-drained soil rich in organic matter.

GROWING METHOD

Propagation Divide existing clumps after the foliage has died down and then replant divisions about 15–20 cm apart. Named varieties must be divided but the species can also be grown from seed sown in autumn.

Watering Needs regular, deep watering through spring and summer.

Fertilising Apply blood and bone as growth commences in spring. Mulch the area with cow manure or compost but don't cover the crown.

Problems No specific pest or disease problems are known for this plant.

FLOWERING

Season Flowers appear in spring, generally before the leaves. They last well and the display is prolonged by the pretty, silky seed heads.

Cutting Flowers are unsuitable for cutting.

AFTER FLOWERING

Requirements Plants should be left alone until the seed heads have faded or fallen. Cut off spent stems and as the plant dies back trim off remaining foliage.

PATERSONIA
Patersonia

THE DELICATE FLOWERS of patersonia each last only a day but plant a clump and flowers will appear day after day for many months.

PATERSONIA, like most flowers, grows best in conditions that mimic its natural environment, in this case in rockeries or well-drained soil.

FEATURES

These small, evergreen Australian perennials belong to the iris family. The most commonly grown species, *P. glabrata*, forms a clump of grassy leaves 15–20 cm high but other species, such as *P. occidentalis* and *P. sericea*, may grow 30 cm or more high. Clumps can spread to about 30 cm wide. The deep lavender to purple, three-petalled flowers last only one day but are borne in a long succession through spring and summer. Patersonia should be planted in pockets in a rockery or at the front of a garden bed so that it is not obscured by larger plants. It can also be grown in a container. All the species seem to be known as native iris in their own districts.

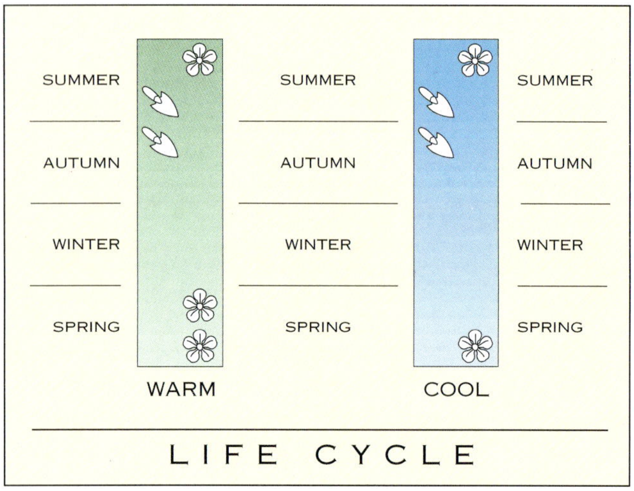

CONDITIONS

Climate Adapts to a range of climates from the subtropics to cool areas. Tolerates a few degrees of frost.

Aspect Prefers full sun but tolerates partial shade or dappled sunlight.

Soil Needs well-drained soil that contains some well-decayed organic matter.

GROWING METHOD

Propagation This is best grown from seed sown in late summer or autumn. Space the plants some 20–30 cm apart.

Watering Although tolerant of dry periods patersonia is best with some deep watering during dry spring and summer weather.

Fertilising Fertiliser is not essential but a little slow release fertiliser can be applied to these plants in spring.

Problems No specific pest and disease problems are known to attack patersonia.

FLOWERING

Season Flowers appear in succession during the spring and summer months.

Cutting Flowers are not suitable for cutting.

AFTER FLOWERING

Requirements The whole plant benefits from being cut back hard after flowering.

PELARGONIUM

Pelargonium* x *domesticum

MANY VARIETIES of pelargonium are available today, giving a rich range of colour and markings, including striking bicolours.

THE CENTREPIECE of this urn is a strong pink pelargonium, standing out from the masses of Swan River daisies around the edge.

FEATURES

AUTUMN WINTER SPRING SUMMER
EVERGREEN

Also known as the regal pelargonium, this evergreen perennial has a shrubby, branching habit. In the United States it is known as the Lady Washington or Martha Washington pelargonium. It grows from 70 cm to 1.5 m tall and the leaves are fluted and slightly hairy. They have a most distinctive spicy smell. The flowers are usually large, with a distinct blotch or feathering on the petals. The colour range includes white, pink, salmon, scarlet, crimson, mauve and purple, with many bicolours and even tricolours.

Uses This is a good plant to include with mixed shrubs or to mass plant in groups of one colour. It also makes a good container plant. A grouping of pots containing pelargoniums would look good on a balcony and be very practical as pelargoniums can stand the exposure. Pelargonium is an easy plant to grow in a hot, sunny position.

CONDITIONS

Climate Prefers a hot, dry climate but can be grown in a range of warm and cool climates. In cold areas keep it frost-free in winter. It does not do well in humid tropical zones.

Aspect Prefers full sun all day.

Soil Grows in almost any well-drained soil. Very acid soils may need additional lime. If growing plants in containers, use a free-draining, good quality potting mix and add 1 teaspoon of lime or dolomite to the mix in a 20 cm pot.

GROWING METHOD

Propagation Tip cuttings taken at almost any time of year strike readily but autumn is probably the best time. New plants should be spaced about 40–50 cm apart. If plants are to be grown in a container, you will find a 20 cm pot is suitable for one growing season.

MANY PELARGONIUM CULTIVARS show this feathering of colour on the petals with a central blotch in a deeper colour.

PELARGONIUMS ARE well adapted to growing in containers but they are even easier to cultivate in the garden.

Watering Water regularly to establish. Once plants are established this is a very drought tolerant plant and it is better underwatered than overwatered. However, an occasional deep soaking will maintain its best appearance.

Fertilising In poor soil apply complete plant food or slow release granules in spring.

Problems • Regal pelargoniums are not attacked by rust in the way geraniums are. Most problems occur when plants are overwatered or where drainage is poor.

LIFE CYCLE

• Caterpillars can sometimes chew leaves and flowers. Search for and destroy them or spray with *Bacillus thuringiensis*.

• Pelargoniums are sometimes badly attacked by sap-sucking whiteflies. Adults, like tiny white moths, rise in a cloud when disturbed and the undersides of the leaf can be thickly covered with nymphs. Small populations can be ignored. There is a wasp that parasitises the nymphs which turn black. Spraying is rather ineffective. Trap adults on a sticky trap available from nurseries or make one yourself. Use a bright yellow board at least 25 cm square and coat it with clean motor oil or something similar. Insects are attracted to the colour and get stuck. Clean the board and recoat it every few days.

FLOWERING

Season Best flowering is mid-spring to early summer but there may be some blooms at other times.

Cutting This is not a good cut flower.

AFTER FLOWERING

Requirements Tip prune after flowering and then cut back hard in autumn to promote vigorous new growth. Re-propagate every three years or so.

PEONY

Paeonia species and cultivars

GLORIOUS COLOUR and perfume combine in this extensive planting of peony cultivars to produce a spectacular result.

THIS HALF-OPENED peony flower gives a hint of delights to come, with a touch of white against the bright pink.

FLUTED PETALS give extra interest to this single white peony. The large mass of central stamens adds a touch of colour.

FEATURES

Beautiful to look at and fragrant too, peonies are among the aristocrats of the plant world, and although there are only thirty-three wild species, there are many hundreds of cultivars. Peonies were prized by the Chinese for many hundreds of years, and by the early eighteenth century they had developed the garden peonies from which the forms of *P. lactiflora* (often referred to as Chinese peonies) are generally descended. Peonies were first introduced into Europe in the late eighteenth century. Peonies are broadly classed into two groups: the tree peonies, which are shrubby and derived from *P. suffruticosa*, and the herbaceous peonies of which the cultivars of *P. lactiflora* are most commonly grown. Although the name 'tree peony' is used, they rarely grow more than 2 m in height. Herbaceous peonies grow about 1 m high and wide. Plants are long lived. Foliage and stems may be reddish when young but mature to a rich green.

Flowers Flowers may be single or double and come in every shade of pink, red, purple, white and cream, many with a delicious light perfume. Some flowers have a large central boss of golden stamens, some have fringed or crimped edges on the petals. Among the categories of flowers recognised are single, double and anemone-flowered. Other categories have been developed in the United States where a great deal of hybridising has been done.

CONDITIONS

Climate Grows best in a cool to cold climate. Some may flower in warmer areas but not unless there is sufficient chilling to ensure complete dormancy for at least two months.

Aspect Needs full sun or semi-shade with protection from strong wind.

Soil Soil must be well drained but heavily enriched with manure or compost. Dig it over deeply to allow free spread of the roots.

THE ATTRACTIVE FOLIAGE greatly adds to the value of peonies in the garden and provides a perfect background for the flowers.

THE VERY POPULAR double cultivar 'Rubra Plena' is a rich crimson anemone-centred peony that looks very like a camellia.

GROWING METHOD

Propagation Divide plants in autumn, taking care not to break the brittle roots. Each division must have roots and dormant growth buds. Crowns should be replanted 2–3 cm below the surface and spaced about 50 cm apart. Plants can be raised from seed but they will take four to five years to reach flowering stage and will not be true to type. Peony seeds generally need two periods of chilling with a warm period between and care should be taken not to disturb the seeds during this time. Most seeds germinate the second spring after sowing.

Watering Needs regular, deep soakings through spring and summer.

Fertilising Apply blood and bone in early spring. At the same time mulch generously with cow manure but avoid the crown area.

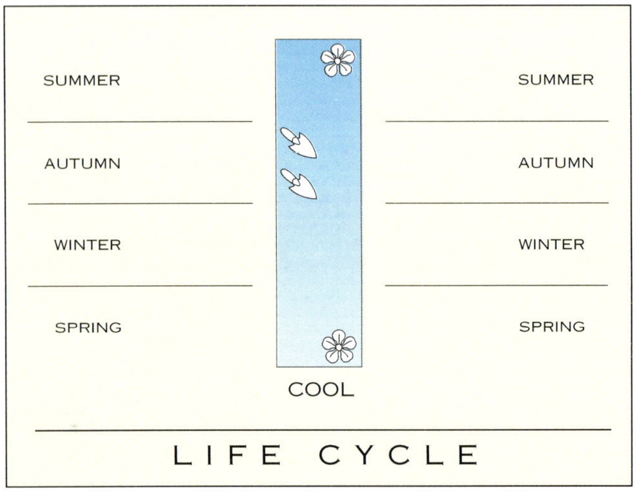

Problems Botrytis or grey mould is the main problem for peonies. It can cause rotting of stems and leaf bases. Destroy affected foliage, improve drainage and air circulation and spray with a registered fungicide. Replace the top layer of soil around the plants.

FLOWERING

Season The flowering period is mid-spring to early summer. Some peonies bloom for only a short time, but the flowers on other types are much longer lasting.

Cutting Cut flowers for indoor use just as the blooms are opening. Peonies are excellent cut flowers, which will last longer if kept in a cool part of the house and given frequent water changes.

AFTER FLOWERING

Requirements Remove spent flower stems but allow the foliage to die down naturally before trimming it back. Some varieties produce lovely autumn colour. If growth is straggly, tip pruning may be increased after the first main flowering. Cut back much harder then on the lower part of the plant stem.

HINT

More flowers Peonies may flower poorly if at all the first year after planting but this should improve year by year. Clumps are best left undisturbed for at least five years and up to ten years. Poor flowering may also result from poor soil. Applying well-rotted cow manure will help.

Perennial Phlox

Phlox paniculata

THE INDIVIDUAL FLOWERS in the flower heads of perennial phlox are the same shape as the flowers of annual phlox.

A GREAT STANDBY for the summer garden, perennial phlox fills the whole of the back of this border with two shades of pink.

FEATURES

Easy to grow and producing a summer-long display of flowers, perennial phlox has a place in any perennial collection. Plants may grow from 40 to 90 cm high and the clumps spread rapidly so that new plantings should be spaced 30 cm or more apart. The large heads of flowers, some with a contrasting eye, come in shades of red, pink, orange, mauve, purple and white. This plant looks best mass planted, either in solid blocks of one colour or in mixed colours. With mixed plantings make sure that the taller forms do not obscure the shorter ones. This plant can be a major feature of a perennial border or used as a background to summer annuals.

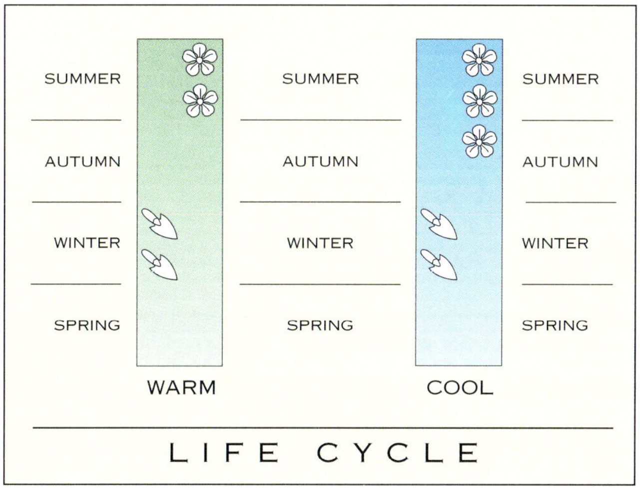

CONDITIONS

Climate Grows in a wide range of cool and warm climates but not in the tropics.

Aspect Prefers full sun with some protection from strong wind.

Soil Needs a well-drained soil enriched with organic matter.

GROWING METHOD

Propagation Divide clumps in winter every three or four years, making sure that each division has a crown and some roots. Replant only the younger, outer growths.

Watering Needs regular, deep watering through spring and summer.

Fertilising Apply complete plant food in spring and mulch well with old cow manure but don't cover the crowns.

Problems No specific pest or disease problems are known to attack this plant.

FLOWERING

Season There is a long flowering period through summer into early autumn.

Cutting It does not make a good cut flower.

AFTER FLOWERING

Requirements Remove spent flower stems as they fade. In late autumn or early winter cut off any remaining growth just above the ground.

PERUVIAN LILY

Alstroemeria

ALSO KNOWN AS lily of the Incas, Peruvian lily can be placed in a mixed perennial border as it is here, or planted between shrubs. Home gardeners can choose from a reasonable range of species and cultivars but they may be unable to obtain many of the varieties sold by florists.

FEATURES

Peruvian lily is grown commercially on a large scale as the flowers are long lasting and very versatile when cut. In the garden it is a herbaceous perennial with flower spikes growing mostly 30–60 cm high, although there are dwarf forms and very tall ones. The flowers are beautifully marked with streaks and spots of colour, contrasting with a wide range of base colours of cream, yellow, orange, pink and red. If conditions suit, these plants spread by means of fleshy rhizomes (roots) to form large clumps. This is a lovely addition to any garden planting and it can also be grown in pots or tubs.

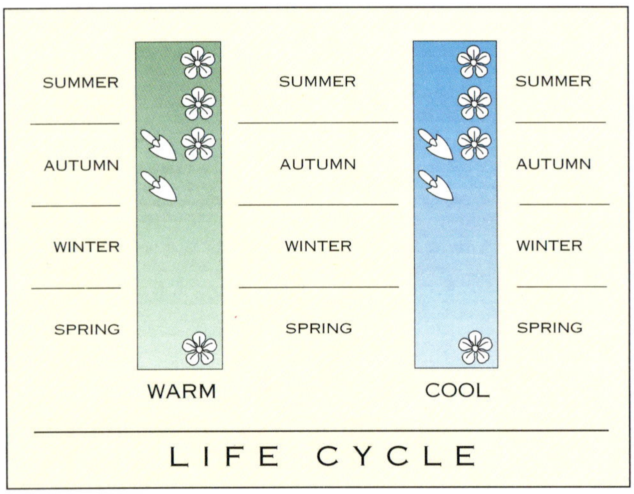

CONDITIONS

Climate Unsuitable for tropics; grows in warm and cool zones. In cold areas grows only in glasshouses.

Aspect Grows in aspects ranging from full sun in cool areas to semi-shade in warm zones. Needs shelter from strong wind.

Soil Must have very free-draining soil containing plenty of decayed organic matter.

GROWING METHOD

Propagation Many grow readily from seed sown in autumn or spring but division of established clumps is easiest. There is some variation with species but autumn is the preferred time for dividing. Plant roots 5 cm deep and about 15 cm apart.

Watering Water regularly in spring and summer but restrict watering after flowering.

Fertilising Apply slow release granular fertiliser in spring. Over-fertilising produces only lots of foliage.

Problems No specific problems are known.

FLOWERING

Season Most species and their cultivars flower from spring into summer, some into autumn.

Cutting This is a first-class cut flower, that lasts longer if stems are scalded before arranging.

AFTER FLOWERING

Requirements Cut off spent flower stems at ground level.

PINKS
Diánthus cultivars

A POPULAR EDGING PLANT for many years, 'Nancy Coleman' has lovely bright pink flowers that fully justify the plant's name.

ONE OF THE BEST pinks for the garden or for use as a cut flower, 'Doris' is vigorous, long flowering and sweetly scented.

FEATURES

Pinks are crosses of *D. caryophyllus* (carnation) and *D. plumarius* (cottage pink) and Allwoods Nurseries in Britain has bred an enormous range of cultivars that are very free-flowering in the right climate. The grey-green foliage grows in a tufted mat and flowering stems are 10–30 cm high. Most flowers are heavily scented and may be single or bicoloured, some with a clear margin of contrasting colour. Most are white, pink, red, deep crimson or salmon. The enormous range of size and form includes small compact varieties ideal for the rock garden. Pinks can be used as edging plants or as components of a mixed border.

CONDITIONS

Climate Prefers a cool to cold winter and dry summer. Grows in warmer areas with low humidity.

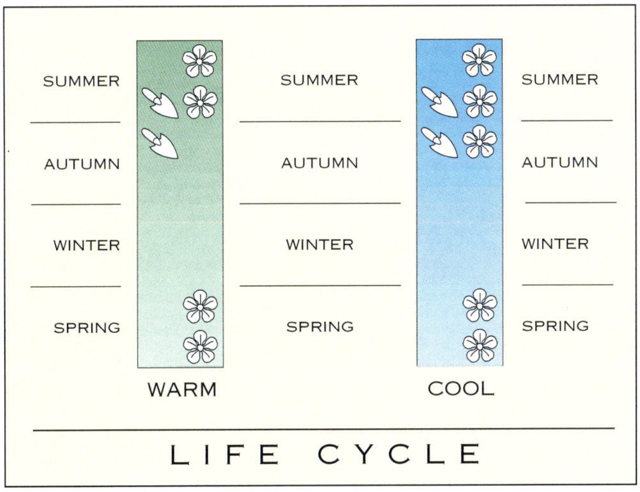

Aspect Needs full sun all day and protection from strong wind.

Soil Needs very free draining soil enriched with decayed organic matter well ahead of planting. On acid soils add about 100 g of lime per square metre before planting.

GROWING METHOD

Propagation Grows easily from cuttings taken in late summer and autumn. Start fresh plants every three or four years to keep vigorous compact growth. Space them 15–30 cm apart, depending on variety.

Watering Water regularly to establish, then give an occasional deep watering in dry spring and summer weather. Never overwater and avoid overhead watering where possible.

Fertilising Apply complete plant food in early spring.

Problems Most diseases of carnations and pinks occur mainly in warm, humid districts. The most upsetting pest is budworm, which bores into the unopened flower bed. Control is difficult because sprays cannot kill the pest once it is inside the bud. Try spraying with *Bacillus thuringiensis* or carbaryl.

FLOWERING

Season Some pinks flower during spring only, others have a long flowering period from spring to early autumn.

Cutting Pinks make excellent cut flowers, providing indoor decoration and scent.

AFTER FLOWERING

Requirements Cut off spent flower stems as they fade. No other pruning is necessary.

Primrose

Primula vulgaris

A CARPET OF PALE YELLOW PRIMROSES is one of the simplest ways of announcing the arrival of spring in the garden. Given a cool, sheltered spot they will thrive and multiply year by year even if they receive very little attention.

FEATURES

This is the true primrose of European woodlands. The species generally has soft, pale yellow flowers tucked in among the leaves on very short stalks although occasionally white or palest pink forms are found. Cultivars come in a huge range of colours with either single or double flowers, some on short stalks, others on quite tall ones. This is one of the parent plants of what we know as polyanthus. Primroses look their best mass planted under deciduous trees or in drifts at the front of a lightly shaded garden bed or perennial border. They can also be grown well in pots. Plants grow from about 10 to 15 cm high with flowering stems about the same height.

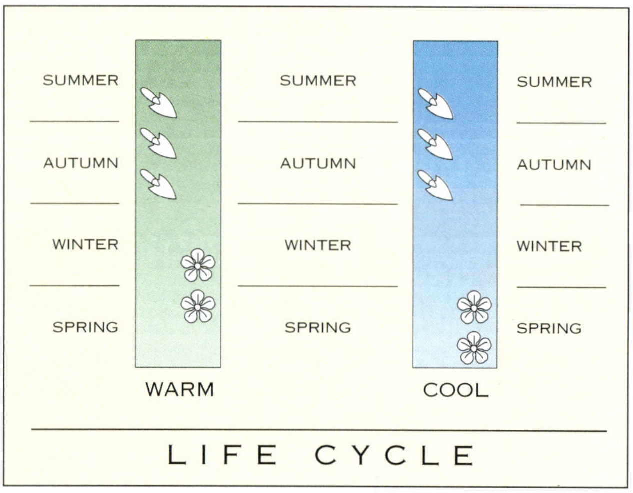

CONDITIONS

Climate Grows most easily in a cool climate but can be grown in a cool spot in warmer areas.

Aspect Prefers to grow in semi-shade and must have protection from summer sun.

Soil Grows best in a medium to heavy moisture-retentive soil heavily enriched with organic matter. Mulch around plants in spring.

GROWING METHOD

Propagation Grows from seed sown in late summer and barely covered, or by dividing established clumps as they become dormant during summer to autumn. Plant 10–15 cm apart.

Watering During spring and summer keep the soil slightly damp. Provide mulch to help retain moisture around plants during dormancy.

Fertilising Apply a little blood and bone or complete plant food in early spring.

Problems No specific problems are known.

FLOWERING

Season Flowering usually lasts for several weeks during late winter into spring, depending on district. Dead-heading prolongs the blooming.

Cutting Flower stems are usually too short for picking.

AFTER FLOWERING

Requirements In suitable conditions plants may self-seed. Remove dead leaves around the plant base.

PURPLE CONEFLOWER

Echinacea purpurea

BOLDER THAN many perennials, coneflowers are sometimes slow to appear in spring but they are well worth the wait.

THIS FINE STAND of bright purple coneflowers adds a striking touch to this entry. The flowers fade as they age but petals don't fall.

FEATURES

Native to the prairie states of the United States, purple coneflower is a hardy, drought resistant plant. Its dark, cone-shaped centre is surrounded by rich, dusty pink ray petals and there are cultivars available in shades of pink-purple and white. They make excellent cut flowers. Purple coneflower often grows over 1 m high, and it is a great addition to a perennial border as it blooms over a long period from late summer into autumn when many other plants have finished. Ideally it should be mass planted to get the best effect. Regular cutting or dead-heading prolongs the floral display. Purple coneflower has a wide range of uses as a medicinal herb and research continues into its potential to increase the body's resistance to infection.

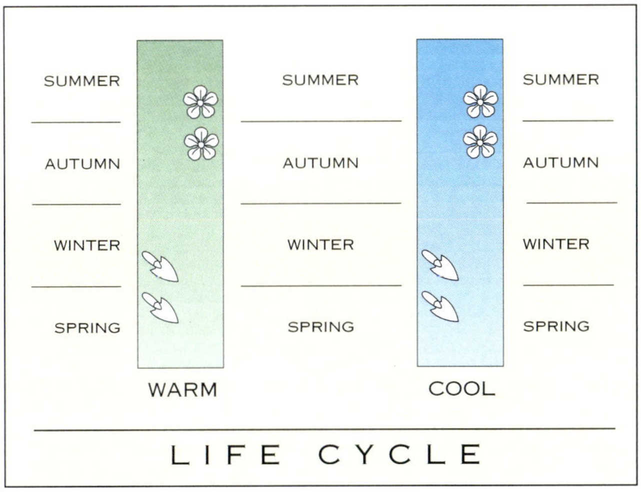

CONDITIONS

Climate Not suitable for the tropics but adaptable to a wide range of cool and warm zones.

Aspect Prefers full sun all day. Although it is tolerant of windy conditions, the blooms will have a better appearance if plants are sheltered from strong wind.

Soil Needs well-drained soil of average quality. Poor or sandy soils can be improved by digging in compost or manure before planting.

GROWING METHOD

Propagation Divide existing clumps in late winter or early spring and replant divisions 20–25 cm apart. It can be grown from seed sown in early spring, which may produce colour variations.

Watering Needs regular water to establish, but then occasional deep soakings in very dry weather are enough, as it tolerates dry conditions well.

Fertilising Apply complete plant food in early spring and again in early summer.

Problems No specific problems are known.

FLOWERING

Season There is a long flowering period from late summer into autumn.

Cutting Cut flowers for the vase when fully open but before the petals separate out.

AFTER FLOWERING

Requirements Remove spent flower stems. The whole plant can be cut back to ground level in winter.

RED HOT POKER

Kniphofia species and cultivars

FLAME COLOURED 'POKERS' and soft purple perovskia both tolerate dry conditions.

THE COLOURS in this generous planting of red hot pokers reflect both the yellow milfoil behind and the red plants in the foreground. The abundant grassy foliage provides useful green contrast.

FEATURES

These evergreen perennials, also known as torch lilies, make great feature plants with their bright flower spikes in cream, orange, red, yellow and many shadings of these colours. Flower stems stand high above the grassy foliage, which may be anywhere from 60 cm to 2 m high. Even out of flower the distinctive foliage makes red hot poker a good accent plant and if space permits several should be planted together. Clumps should remain undisturbed for many years, so choose the planting position with care.

CONDITIONS

Climate Not suitable for the tropics but should do well in all other warm and cool areas. Tolerates a wide range of exposed windy or coastal sites.

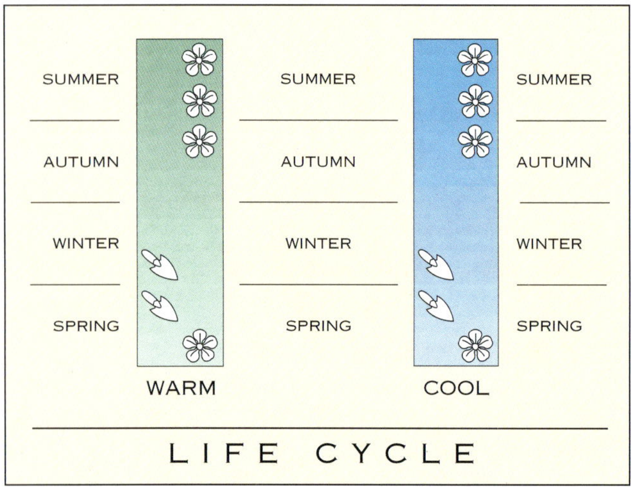

Aspect Needs full sun all day.

Soil Needs well-drained soil. Although it tolerates poorer soils, you will get better results if the soil is enriched with manure or compost.

GROWING METHOD

Propagation Existing well-established clumps can be divided in late winter or early spring. Foliage on new divisions must be reduced by half to allow successful root regrowth. Smaller growing forms can be planted at 50 cm spacings but large growers may need up to 80 cm or more.

Watering Needs regular watering to establish but once established is very drought tolerant. However, if water is plentiful give an occasional deep watering during flowering.

Fertilising Grows without supplementary fertiliser but complete plant food applied in spring should increase the quality of the flowers.

Problems No specific problems are known.

FLOWERING

Season Flowering times vary with species or cultivar. Many red hot pokers flower in late spring through summer or summer into autumn, but there are several species that bloom from midwinter to spring.

Cutting Flowers last well when cut if the stems are scalded for 10 seconds or so.

AFTER FLOWERING

Requirements Spent flower stalks should be cut off. Any dead leaves should be pulled out to give the clump a clean look. Chop dead leaves and use as mulch.

RED VALERIAN

Centranthus ruber

TRUSSES of rich crimson and softer pink valerian provide months of colour in the garden without the work associated with annuals.

RED VALERIAN flourishes here in the conditions that suit it best: the fence provides shelter, the raised bed perfect drainage.

FEATURES

EVERGREEN

This evergreen perennial is very easy to grow but it often exceeds its allotted space by self-sowing in other parts of the garden. It is capable of gaining a foothold almost anywhere. It is, however, easy to pull out. It has a very long flowering period and can survive in poor, dry soil where other plants would fail. Mostly seen around 40 cm high, in good soil it can grow to around 70 cm. Flowers are a deep pink to red and there is a white form, too. Ideal for a low maintenance garden, it is often planted in mixed borders for its long floral display. It is also grown in large rockeries or on dry, fast-draining slopes. Self-sown plants can be found in almost no soil on rock outcrops.

CONDITIONS

Climate Grows well almost anywhere except in the tropical zones.

Aspect Prefers full sun all day.

Soil Needs very well-drained soil but it need not be particularly rich.

GROWING METHOD

Propagation Grows readily from tip cuttings taken in late spring and summer or from seed sown in spring. Space plants about 20 cm apart.

Watering Needs regular water to establish but then plants are extremely drought tolerant. However, plants respond well to occasional deep watering during spring and summer.

Fertilising Fertiliser is generally not necessary but you may give a little complete plant food in spring.

Problems No specific problems are known.

FLOWERING

Season The very long flowering period extends from spring until early autumn, especially if plants are cut back after each flowering flush.

Cutting This is not a good vase flower.

AFTER FLOWERING

Requirements No attention is needed beyond removal of spent flower stems. Cutting spent flowers off before they have set seed will avoid the spread of plants into places where they are unwanted.

Rock Rose

Helianthemum nummularium

THE DEEP RED FLOWERS of 'Supreme' stand out against the grey-green foliage.

SEVERAL VARIETIES of rock rose are combined here to form a mini-hedge that serves to camouflage the bare lower stems of the tall roses behind.

FEATURES

Rock rose, or sun rose, makes a spreading mound that may reach 1 m wide in ideal conditions. Plants are evergreen and only 10–30 cm high but in the long flowering period are smothered in flat, rounded flowers. Flowers may be single or double and the colour range includes many shades of yellow, pink, red, orange, white and terracotta. They tend to close if the light levels are low. Rock rose can be grown at the front of a border, on top of low walls, in rockeries or pots. It is not long lived but easily raised from cuttings.

CONDITIONS

Climate Grows in cool to cold zones. Prefers areas of low humidity.

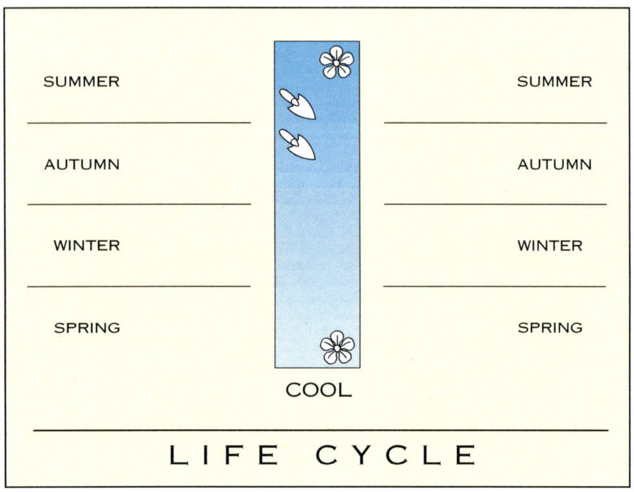

Aspect Must have full sun all day.

Soil Needs very well-drained and slightly alkaline soil. Add lime or dolomite, 100 g per square metre, to soils known to be very acid.

GROWING METHOD

Propagation Take cuttings of semi-hardwood lateral growths in summer or early autumn. Plant at about 30 cm intervals for quick effect. These should make flowering-sized plants by the following spring.

Watering Water regularly to establish. Once plants are established, give them an occasional heavy watering if conditions are very dry.

Fertilising Give a light application of pelletted poultry manure in spring.

Problems Poor drainage or overwatering will kill plants. Powdery mildew may be a problem in humid districts. To deter it, improve air circulation if plants are crowded and avoid watering late in the day.

FLOWERING

Season The main flowering period is from mid-spring to midsummer, but if plants are sheared off after the first flush there may be a second flush of blooms.

Cutting Flowers are not suitable for cutting.

AFTER FLOWERING

Requirements Trim over the plant to remove spent blooms. A light trim in late winter or early spring helps to keep plants compact and will improve the flowering.

SALVIA

Salvia

*MEALY CUP SAGE (*Salvia farinacea*) is native to the south-west of the United States and so is very tolerant of dry conditions. This spectacular large-scale planting of both purple and white types could be copied on a smaller scale in the home garden.*

FEATURES

Salvias are a huge plant group of over 700 species comprising shrubs, herbaceous perennials and annuals. Most people associate salvias with red or purple flowers but there are also species with cream, yellow, white, blue or pink flowers. Many have highly aromatic foliage with scents ranging from the delicious to the outright unpleasant: the foliage of pineapple sage, *S. elegans* (syn. *S. rutilans*) has a delicious perfume while the bog sage (*S. uliginosa*) smells rather unpleasant. Most salvias are extremely easy to grow and once established need little attention beyond occasional deep watering in hot weather and some cutting back after flowering. The tall salvias are ideal for the back of the border or for fillers between shrubs. There are many others of varying heights that are suitable as edging plants or for planting among annuals, bulbs and other perennials. Mealy cup sage, *S. farinacea*, has deep purple or white flowers with a white, woolly coating—this grows 30–50 cm high, is short lived and often better treated as an annual.

Culinary sage Culinary sage, *S. officinalis*, is one of the salvias. It has grey, rather wrinkly foliage and flowers that are usually pale violet. Despite its desirability, it is often one of the most difficult of the salvias to grow as it demands perfect drainage and dislikes both humidity and too much summer rain.

Others *S. involucrata*, a vigorous, easy-to-grow garden plant, grows to about 1.2 m and has bright rosy pink flowers over a very long period. *S. microphylla* has bright red flowers, while there are the most intense deep blue flowers on *S. patens*, *S. guaranitica* and *S. azurea*. All of these grow in excess of 1 m. Two other very useful perennials in the garden are Mexican sage, *S. leucantha*, and bog sage, *S. uliginosa*. Both have long flowering periods. Mexican sage has grey-green leaves and bears its velvety purple flowers through autumn and into winter. Bog sage has bright blue flowers with a touch of white and blooms through summer into autumn. This can be somewhat invasive, but unwanted plants are readily pulled out. Both species are very vigorous, growing 1.5–2 m tall and spreading rapidly by means of their underground stems.

CONDITIONS

Climate Unsuitable for the tropics but salvia is quite easy to grow in a wide range of both cool and warm climates.

Aspect Many species prefer to be in full sun all day but quite a number tolerate semi-shade or shade for part of the day. Several of these can be grown in dappled shade under trees.

Soil Any well-drained soil is suitable. Mulching with decayed manure in early spring improves the soil condition.

*MEXICAN SAGE (*Salvia leucantha*) needs plenty of room to spread and is ideally placed here in the fast-draining soil beside a gravel drive. Its long autumn flowering lasts into winter.*

MANY SALVIAS have blue flowers. This cultivar of mealy cup sage is 'Russian Blue'.

GROWING METHOD

Propagation Grows from seed sown in spring or cuttings taken in late summer through autumn. Many species grow from rooted divisions of an established clump. Lift a clump and you will find numerous pieces with both roots and shoots. Divisions can be made from autumn until spring. Plant out the divisions about 25 cm apart.

Watering Needs regular watering to establish. Once established, plants can be very drought tolerant although an occasional deep soaking in dry times will produce better growth and more abundant blooming.

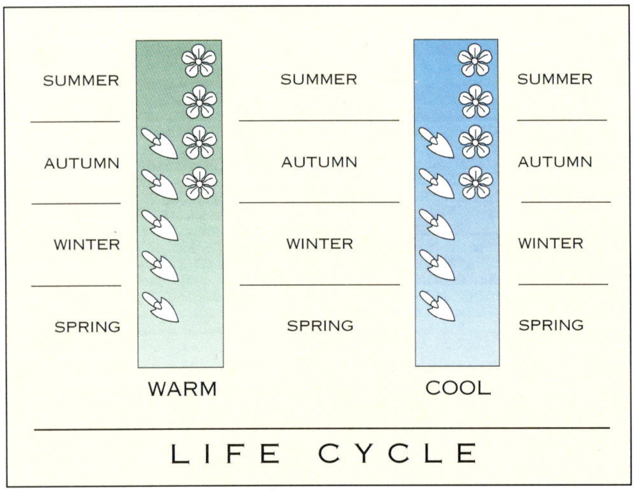

Fertilising Complete plant food or pelletted poultry manure can be applied in spring in poor soil but too much fertiliser will result in all foliage and few flowers.

Problems No specific problems are known but poorly drained soils and overwatering may kill plants.

FLOWERING

Season Many salvias have a very long flowering period. Many species flower through summer into autumn while there are very useful autumn-flowering species such as *S. leucantha* that flower through until early winter. The species that flower from summer to autumn are especially useful as they continue to bloom after many perennials have finished.

Cutting None of these salvias makes a good cut flower but their long, dependable flowering season makes them a great asset in any garden.

AFTER FLOWERING

Requirements Plants can be tip pruned after each flowering flush to promote further blooming. In late autumn or early winter plants can be cut off just above ground level. If you do not want to lift and divide a clump you can wait until new growth starts in spring and simply thin out growth that is too crowded. A number of perennial salvias are extremely vigorous but just pull out plants or running roots whenever they are getting out of bounds.

Sea Lavender

Limonium latifolium

FLOWER HEADS of sea lavender are made up of myriads of tiny little flowers.

SEA LAVENDER has broad, slightly fleshy leaves, here growing in total contrast to the shrubby Mexican orange blossom behind it. Sea lavender flowers can last several months in the garden.

FEATURES

Sea lavender is a perennial type of statice often grown simply for its tall, finely branched stems of tiny white and pale lavender flowers, which are widely used both in fresh and dried floral arrangements. Flower stems may be over 50 cm high and there are cultivars, including 'Rosea' with pinkish flowers and 'Violetta' with deeper violet flowers. The plant forms a basal rosette of broad, rounded, slightly fleshy leaves growing around 25 cm high. Clumps may ultimately spread 60 cm or more wide. This is a good plant for rockeries or borders, including dry borders, as it is quite drought tolerant once established. Sea lavender is native to parts of south-eastern and central Europe where it thrives in hot, dry summers and cold winters.

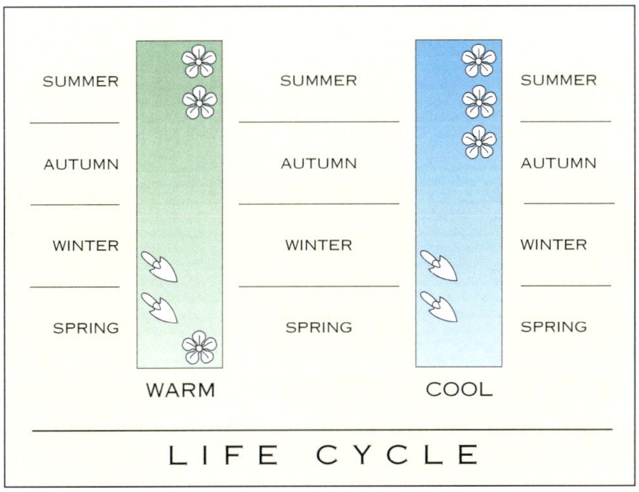

CONDITIONS

Climate Unsuitable for tropics but grows in warm and cool districts if summer humidity is not high.

Aspect Prefers full sun all day and tolerates exposed windy or coastal sites.

Soil Soil must be very well drained but need not be rich. Sea lavender tolerates very poor soil.

GROWING METHOD

Propagation Grows from seed sown as soon as it is ripe when the flowers have dried and browned off, or from root cuttings taken in winter to early spring. New plantings should be spaced about 25–30 cm apart.

Watering Water regularly to establish and then give occasional deep soakings during very dry spring and summer weather.

Fertilising Does not need fertilising but a little complete plant food may be applied in early spring.

Problems Heavy, poorly drained soils or overwatering may cause the plant to rot and collapse.

FLOWERING

Season Sea lavender has a long flowering period, from mid-spring through summer in warm areas or from summer to early autumn in cool areas.

Cutting Flowers can be cut for drying when most of the flowers on the stem are fully open.

AFTER FLOWERING

Requirements Cut off faded flower stems if they have not already been removed for indoor decoration.

Shasta Daisy

Leucanthemum* x *superbum*, syn. *Chrysanthemum maximum

LONG-STEMMED shasta daisies are an ideal component of flower arrangements.

A CONTINUOUS PLANTING of shasta daisies fills this awkward narrow space between a path and a low brick wall. The cheerful white flowers appear throughout summer.

FEATURES

Shasta daisies look wonderful when planted in a mixed border where their large white flowers provide the perfect accompaniment to other, more brightly coloured flowers. They are herbaceous but don't die down completely in warm climates, and despite being easy to grow and multiplying rapidly they don't become a menace. Flower stalks can grow 50–60 cm high, while the dark green leaves are only 10–15 cm high. Shasta daisies make great cut flowers. There are a number of named cultivars available, some such as 'Esther Read', 'Wirral Supreme' and 'Cobham Gold' with double flowers. (Despite its name, the flowers on 'Cobham Gold' are cream, not gold.) 'Everest' is probably the largest of the single cultivars. There is an attractive dwarf form suitable for edging beds. Flowers are 25–30 cm high.

CONDITIONS

Climate Grows well in a range of cool to warm climates but not in the tropics.

Aspect Prefers full sun all day and wind protection.

Soil Soil should be well drained and improved by the addition of decayed compost or manure.

GROWING METHOD

Propagation Divide clumps in late winter or early spring, replanting only the younger, outer growths, each with its own roots and shoots. Plant divisions about 25 cm apart.

Watering Needs regular, deep watering through spring and summer for good-sized plants and blooms.

Fertilising Apply complete plant food as growth begins in spring. Liquid fertiliser applied in late spring should help produce better blooms.

Problems Distorted greenish flowers may have a virus known as big bud or virescence. This is carried by sap-sucking leafhoppers. There is no control for this disease which affects a range of plants including some weeds. Affected plants should be discarded. Keep the area weed-free and use insecticidal soap sprays to control insects.

FLOWERING

Season Flowering is from late spring through summer.

Cutting Cut flowers regularly for indoor decoration as this should prolong the display.

AFTER FLOWERING

Requirement Cut off any remaining spent flower stems as low down as possible.

SNEEZEWEED

Helenium autumnale

STILL ONE OF the best and most popular cultivars of sneezeweed, 'Moerheim Beauty' has been around since 1930.

ORANGE AND TAWNY COLOURS are a feature of sneezeweed, a reliable perennial that brightens the autumn garden.

FEATURES

As its Latin name suggests, this herbaceous perennial flowers from late summer through autumn. The straight species has bright golden, daisy-type flowers with dark centres but many of the most popular cultivars have flowers in rich tones of orange-red or copper-red. 'Butterpat', 'Moerheim Beauty' and 'Walstrand' are among the most popular varieties. Sneezeweed can grow 1–1.5 m or more high, eventually forming large clumps over 50 cm across. Flowers cut well but the plant is probably more valuable for its contribution to the autumn garden. It should be placed at the back of a perennial border or among shrubs. Sneezeweed is a native of North America where it grows in marshy ground in open, sunny meadows. It is an easy plant to grow if growing conditions are suitable.

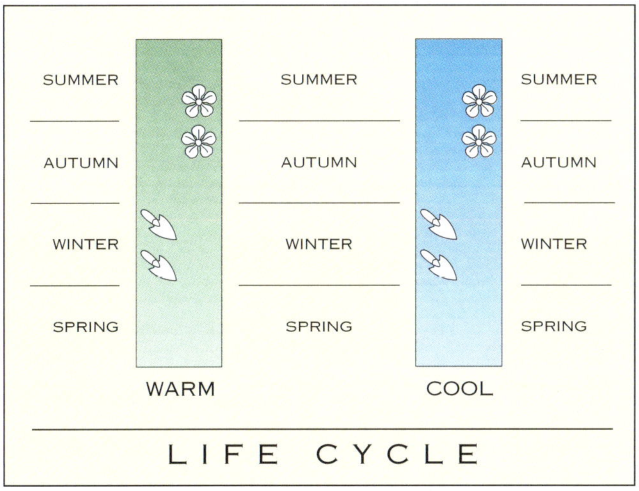

CONDITIONS

Climate Grows in warm and cool districts but prefers cooler areas.

Aspect Needs to be grown in full sun all day.

Soil Needs a moisture-retentive soil heavily enriched with organic matter. It will not thrive in dry soil. Mulch around clumps to help keep soil moist.

GROWING METHOD

Propagation Established clumps can be lifted and divided about every three years. Discard the oldest central sections and replant the divisions about 30 cm apart.

Watering Give regular, thorough watering right through the growing season.

Fertilising Apply complete plant food as new growth commences in spring.

Problems Sneezeweed is generally free from problems although weevils and beetles can damage newly emerging growth in some areas.

FLOWERING

Season The long flowering starts in late summer and continues through autumn.

Cutting Flowers cut well for indoor decoration.

AFTER FLOWERING

Requirements Spent flower stems should be removed. As the plant dies down, cut off dead foliage. It can be chopped and left on the ground as mulch. Flowers bloom into autumn, so foliage may remain in good condition until early winter.

SOLOMON'S SEAL

Polygonatum multiflorum

A HORIZONTAL STEM of pretty white Solomon's seal flowers is suspended above a groundcover of lungwort and dead nettle.

SOLOMON'S SEAL grows tall in this lovely cool climate garden, where it is teamed with hostas, lady's mantle and foxgloves.

FEATURES

This lovely herbaceous perennial is strictly for cool climates. In other areas it may grow but will rarely, if ever, flower. The plant has a graceful, arching habit with stems 60–90 cm long. The finely veined foliage tends to stand up on the stem while the pretty tubular, white bell flowers tipped in green hang down from the stem. This plant is ideal for naturalising in a woodland garden, for planting under deciduous trees or for incorporating into a shady border. It grows from a creeping rhizome and will spread to form a colony of plants. If space is no problem, plant several to start your display. A number of other species are cultivated in cool climate gardens, some, such as *P. odoratum*, with scented flowers.

CONDITIONS

Climate Strictly for cool climate gardens.

Aspect Needs a sheltered spot in part or full shade.

Soil The soil should drain well but be heavily enriched with organic matter to retain some moisture at all times. Plants benefit from mulching too.

GROWING METHOD

Propagation Established clumps can be divided in autumn, new divisions being spaced 20–25 cm apart. This plant is best left undisturbed for several years if possible.

Watering Needs to be watered regularly during the growing season; doesn't tolerate dryness then.

Fertilising Apply complete plant food as new growth commences in spring.

Problems No specific problems are known but slugs and snails may damage newly emerging foliage.

FLOWERING

Season Flowers appear in spring, often fairly late spring in cold areas.

Cutting Flowers can be cut for indoor decoration. They last fairly well.

AFTER FLOWERING

Requirements Nothing special needs to be done although faded flower stems can be cut off. Continue regular watering until the growth starts to brown off.

SPIDERWORT

Tradescantia virginiana

SPIDERWORT FLOWERS look like small purple irises but each lasts only a day. The surrounding buds are waiting their turn to open.

DENSE PLANTINGS of spiderwort produce plenty of flowers and thrive in filtered sunlight where other plants may not be happy.

FEATURES

This North American herbaceous perennial has a number of common names, including widow's tears and trinity flower. It is a spreading plant with tapering, strappy leaves and showy, triangular flowers in rich purple, rose pink or white. The flowers generally last only one day but they appear in succession over a long period. There are several named cultivars available. Spiderwort grows to between 30 and 60 cm high and is multi-stemmed. It is easy to grow in the right conditions and can make a tall groundcover in filtered sunlight under trees. In mild climates it may not die down completely.

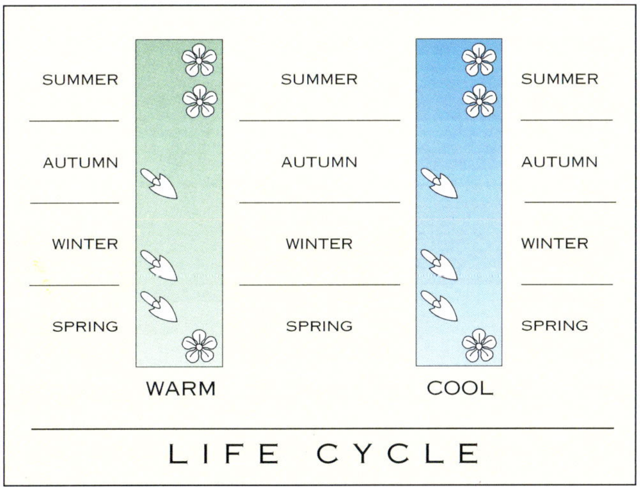

CONDITIONS

Climate Grows in both cool and warm zones but not the tropics.

Aspect Prefers filtered sunlight but can be grown in morning sun and afternoon shade.

Soil Grows best in soil that is well drained but heavily enriched with decayed organic matter.

GROWING METHOD

Propagation Clumps can be lifted and divided in late winter to early spring. The species can be grown from seed sown in autumn. It is occasionally self-sown. New plantings should be 30–45 cm apart, depending on how rapidly you need cover.

Watering Needs regular watering during dry spring and summer weather.

Fertilising Apply blood and bone or complete plant food as growth starts in spring.

Problems No specific problems are known.

FLOWERING

Season The long succession of flowers starts in spring and continues through summer.

Cutting Flowers are unsuitable for cutting.

AFTER FLOWERING

Requirements Growth starts to yellow and die back after flowering. Clean away dead foliage.

STOKES' ASTER

Stokesia laevis

THE FLOWERING HEADS of stokes' aster are quite complex, made up of many 'petals' (more properly bracts or ray florets).

IT IS HARD to understand why the pretty stokes' aster would go out of fashion but it is certainly grown less often than before.

FEATURES

Stokes' aster is an easy to grow plant that provides great decorative value throughout its long flowering period from early summer to mid-autumn. It makes an excellent cut flower, too. Flower stems 30–50 cm high rise from a cluster of dark green basal leaves. Although this plant is completely herbaceous in cold areas, the basal growth remains evergreen in warmer regions. Flowers are reminiscent of large cornflowers or asters, and come in shades of blue, white and mauve. This plant can look outstanding in mass plantings but is equally at home in a mixed border. It is also suitable for container growing and would suit balcony gardeners. In warm regions stokes' aster can be quite vigorous.

CONDITIONS

Climate Prefers warm to subtropical climates but grows in cooler climates with winter protection.

Aspect Prefers full sun but grows in dappled sunlight in warm zones. Protect from strong wind.

Soil Needs well-drained soil enriched with compost or manure.

GROWING METHOD

Propagation Divide established clumps in late winter to early spring, replanting divisions about 25 cm apart. This plant can also be grown from root cuttings taken in late winter and the straight species from autumn-sown seed, although results can be variable.

Watering Tolerates dry periods but looks best if given an occasional deep watering in dry, hot weather. Restrict watering once flowering stops.

Fertilising Apply some complete plant food in spring.

Problems Poorly drained, heavy soils and overwatering induce root or crown rot, which kills plants.

FLOWERING

Season The long flowering period is throughout summer into autumn.

Cutting Cut flowers regularly for the vase as this will help prolong blooming.

AFTER FLOWERING

Requirements Prune off spent flower stems. As growth dies back, clean away dead leaves.

Stone Crop

Sedum spectabile

DENSE FLOWER HEADS of stone crop provide a rich source of nectar, attracting butterflies and other insects to the garden.

BILLOWING HEADS of stone crop add colour to the autumn garden. Here they edge a mixed border, with white beard tongue behind.

FEATURES

One of over 600 species of succulent sedums, this one is unusual in that it is frequently used in perennial plantings where many succulent plants would look out of place. It has fleshy, soft green leaves on stems that may be from 40 to 60 cm high. New growth appears at the base of older stems, and so increasing the stock of plants is easy. The large heads of flowers are a soft mauve-pink in the species but there are a number of cultivars with colours ranging from bright hot pinks through to rosy red and the brick red of 'Autumn Joy'. Depending on climate and district, these plants may be in flower from late spring through summer or through summer into autumn. Stone crop is a very easy plant to care for as it tolerates a wide range of conditions, has few problems and needs little special care.

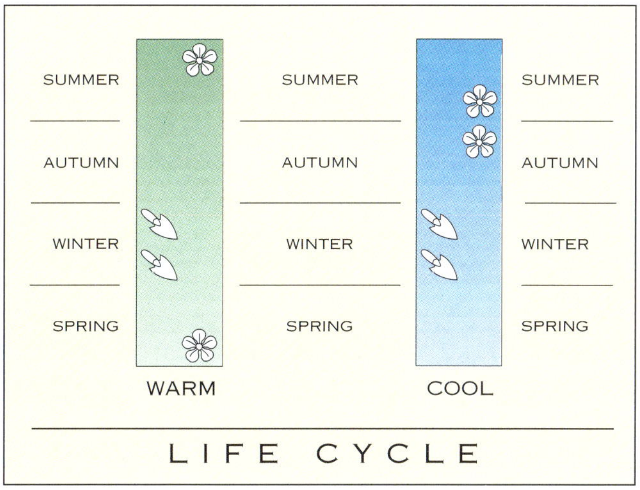

CONDITIONS

Climate Grows in both warm and cool zones but not in the tropics.

Aspect Prefers full sun but tolerates shade for part of the day.

Soil Prefers a sandy, well-drained soil but tolerates heavier soil, which is unusual for sedums.

GROWING METHOD

Propagation Clumps of plants are easily pulled apart in late winter and divisions are replanted at about 15–20 cm intervals. It is also possible to strike this plant from stem cuttings.

Watering Water regularly to establish. Once established, this is drought tolerant but an occasional deep watering in dry, warm weather is beneficial.

Fertilising Slow release fertiliser can be applied in spring. Avoid overfertilising as this may result in sappy leaf growth but fewer flowers.

Problems No specific problems are known.

FLOWERING

Season Flowering may be from late spring through summer or through summer into autumn, depending on the district.

Cutting Flowers last well in the garden but not so in the vase.

AFTER FLOWERING

Requirements Spent flower heads can be snipped off once they have faded completely but it is best to cut stems off 10–15 cm above the ground to force new growth the following season.

Swamp Rose Mallow

Hibiscus moscheutos

AMPLE SUMMER MOISTURE will produce glorious flowers such as this.

PETALS like finely pleated white silk make this swamp rose mallow most attractive.

MASSES OF BUDS show these large, showy blooms will continue for some time.

FEATURES

This species of hibiscus is completely herbaceous, dying right back to the roots even in fairly warm districts. It produces very large single flowers 15–20 cm across, the silky petals being white, various shades of pink or deep crimson—often with a deeper coloured throat. Many of the best strains are sold under the name of 'Southern Belle' or 'Dixie Belle'. Its natural distribution is over most of the eastern United States where it is found in marshland. There it is sometimes known as marsh mallow, sea hollyhock or even wild cotton. It grows up to 1.5 m high with a shrub-like form and should be grown at the back of a border or among other garden shrubs. Although it can be grown alone, several planted together make a real impact.

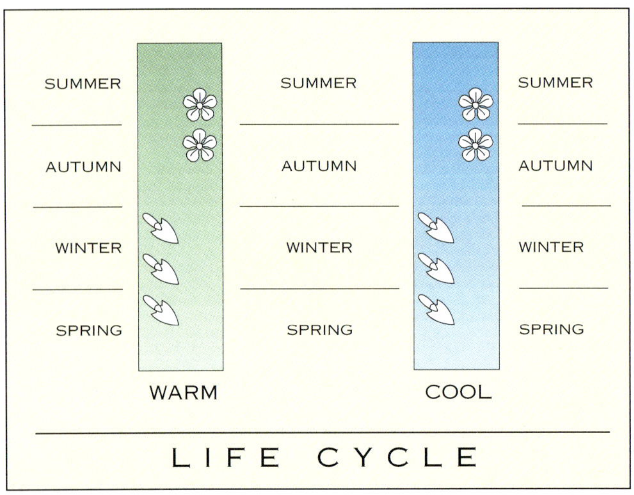

CONDITIONS

Climate Suitable for cool and warm areas.

Aspect Must be grown in full sun, preferably with some wind protection.

Soil Prefers a moisture-retentive soil enriched with organic matter.

GROWING METHOD

Propagation Divide the woody rootstocks in winter or very early spring. This is sometimes difficult but it is also possible to grow this plant from cuttings of the first new shoots in spring.

Watering Needs regular, deep watering during spring and summer.

Fertilising Apply complete plant food as growth begins in spring. Mulch with cow manure or rich compost at the same time.

Problems Swamp rose mallow is generally trouble-free but watch for chewing insects as new growth starts in spring.

FLOWERING

Season Blooms during summer, sometimes into autumn. Like most hibiscus, flowers are not long lasting but they are spectacular.

Cutting Flowers are not suitable for cutting.

AFTER FLOWERING

Requirements Keep removing spent flowers during the season. Allow the plant to die down naturally, cutting back the woody stem only after it has turned brown.

THRIFT

Armeria maritima

EACH FLOWER HEAD resembles a tiny posy, and thrift does indeed make a fine cut flower, whether used alone or with other flowers.

POOR STONY GROUND, which resembles thrift's natural habitat, can provide ideal conditions for growing this plant.

FEATURES

Also known as sea pink, this evergreen perennial grows in little grassy mounds 8–12 cm high. It occurs naturally in northern Europe and around the Mediterranean, often in very exposed situations, including cliff tops. The rounded flower heads are carried above the foliage on stems 15–30 cm high. Flowers vary in colour in the species and may be white, pink or almost red, and there are a number of named cultivars available. Thrift has a very long flowering period if spent flowers are regularly removed. The cut flowers can be used for decoration, either fresh or dried. Thrift can be used as a groundcover or edging plant, or it can be planted in rockeries, on dry walls or in poor soil where most other plants would not survive. It also makes a good container plant.

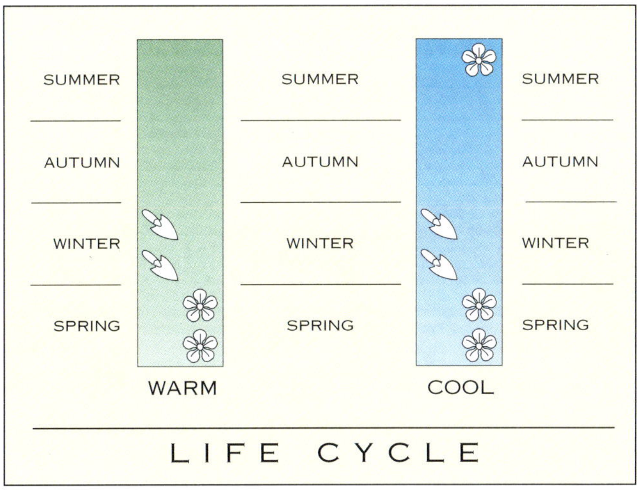

CONDITIONS

Climate Suitable for both cool and warm zones but not the tropics.

Aspect Needs full sun all day. Thrift tolerates dry, windy conditions and salt spray.

Soil Grows in any kind of soil as long as it is very well drained. It does not need rich soil.

GROWING METHOD

Propagation Divide established clumps in winter and replant 15–20 cm apart. The species can be grown from seed sown in spring.

Watering Give an occasional deep watering in dry weather during spring and summer. Do not overwater as the plants will rot quickly.

Fertilising Give a light dressing of complete fertiliser in early spring.

Problems Thrift has a tendency to rot if soils are heavy, poorly drained or overwatered. In humid districts or in sheltered positions it may be susceptible to rust, a fungal disease. Use a fungicide registered for this disease.

FLOWERING

Season Thrift has a long flowering period through spring and summer as long as plants are dead-headed regularly.

Cutting Makes a good cut flower.

AFTER FLOWERING

Requirements Apart from the removal of spent flower stems no other treatment is necessary.

VIOLET

Viola odorata

DESPITE the range of cultivars available, the simple violet species is still the favourite.

VIOLETS PROVIDE great groundcover under deciduous trees or in other shaded, sheltered spots. They do, however, need some sun or flowering will be poor.

FEATURES

Violets have been in cultivation since ancient times and they were valued by the Ancient Greeks as medicinal plants. They were grown in monastery gardens through the Middle Ages and have been written about in poetry and prose for centuries. In Victorian times there was an enormous number of varieties grown, including a wide range of the double Parma violets. The violet's sweet fragrance and simple flowers make them favourites with gardeners and florists alike. Plants have a creeping habit and are rarely more than 15–20 cm high. The deep violet-purple flowers may be on stems up to 20 cm high in good conditions. There are cultivars with single or double flowers in purple, pink, white or bicolours but the deep purple is probably the best loved. There are many other species of delightful violets to grow in cool climate gardens.

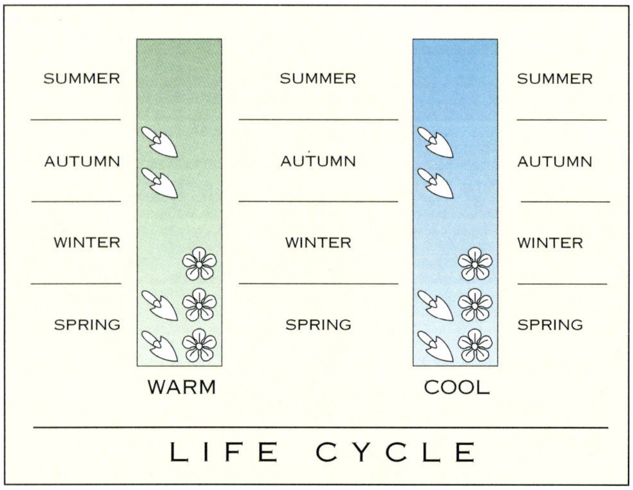

CONDITIONS

Climate Grows best in cool climates but can be grown in cool spots in warm climate gardens.

Aspect Needs shade or dappled sunlight with protection from drying winds. Grows in full sun in cool districts.

Soil Needs well-drained but moisture-retentive soil, heavily enriched with organic matter.

GROWING METHOD

Propagation Clumps can be lifted and divided or runners can be dug up and replanted every couple of years, in autumn or in spring after flowering. Plant at 20 cm spacings with plant crowns just above soil level. Violets self-seed, too.

Watering Keep plants very well watered during spring and summer. They need the water and it helps discourage attack by mites.

Fertilising Apply complete plant food in spring after flowering ceases.

Problems There are two fungal diseases that can attack violets but they are not commonly found in home gardens.

FLOWERING

Season Violets flower from late winter into spring.

Cutting Scalding stems of cut violets before arranging them will increase their vase life.

AFTER FLOWERING

Requirements No special treatment is needed but excess runners can be removed during the growing season if they are invasive or to channel vigour back to the main crowns.

WINTER ROSE

Helleborus

PRETTY SHADINGS of colour are shown on the winter rose. Seedlings often produce unexpected colours, which can be maintained if the plants are then propagated by division.

NATIVE to Corsica and Sardinia, this is green-flowered Helleborus argutifolius.

FEATURES

Various species of hellebores are known as winter rose, or as Christmas or Lenten rose because of their flowering times in the northern hemisphere. They do indeed flower in winter or very early spring. *H. niger*, which has pure white flowers with green centres, is difficult to grow except in very cold climates. *H. argutifolius* (syn. *H. corsicus*) and *H. orientalis* grow happily in warmer areas. *H. argutifolius* has lovely lime-green flowers and very spiny-toothed leaf margins while *H. orientalis* is more variable and may have white, green, pink or mottled flowers. Cultivars include a deep crimson variety. These perennials are mostly evergreen and best planted under deciduous trees where they can remain undisturbed. Some are fairly short lived but they tend to self-seed so that you do not lose them. They range in height from 30 to 60 cm.

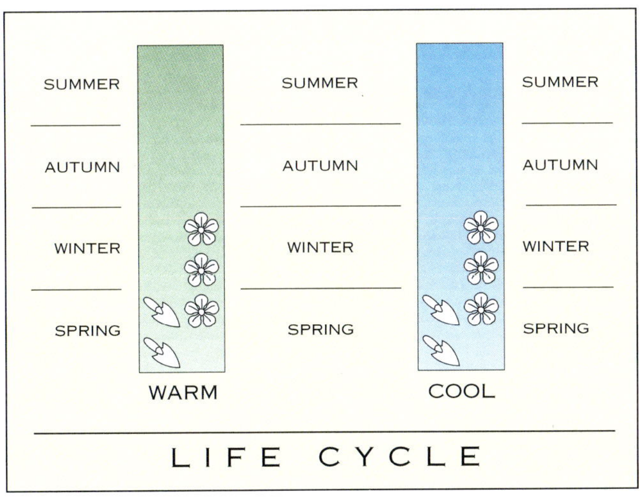

CONDITIONS

Climate Suitable for cool to warm areas only.

Aspect Prefers dappled sunlight under trees or other partially shaded spots.

Soil Soil must be well enriched with organic matter and able to retain moisture.

GROWING METHOD

Propagation Divisions of clumps should be made in spring, straight after flowering, the divisions being replanted about 20–30 cm apart. Seed can be sown in early summer but seedlings will take about three years to flower. Seedlings often produce interesting shades.

Watering Plants need plenty of water and should be given regular, heavy watering during dry periods in spring and summer.

Fertilising Apply a little complete plant food in spring. Mulch each spring with manure or compost to aid moisture retention.

Problems There are no specific problems for winter roses apart from the fact that snails like to graze on the foliage.

FLOWERING

Season The long flowering period is from midwinter to early spring.

Cutting Winter rose makes a lovely cut flower.

AFTER FLOWERING

Requirements Prune off dead flower stems and any dead leaves. Hellebores don't like disturbance, and so apart from mulching and watering, leave them alone.

FLOWERING CHART

PLANT COMMON NAME	SUITABLE CLIMATE	SPRING EARLY	SPRING MID	SPRING LATE	SUMMER EARLY	SUMMER MID	SUMMER LATE	AUTUMN EARLY	AUTUMN MID	AUTUMN LATE	WINTER EARLY	WINTER MID	WINTER LATE
African daisy	🟡🟢🔵	🟡🟢🔵	🟡🟢🔵	🟡🟢🔵	🟡🟢🔵	🔵	🔵						🟡🟢
Agapanthus	🟡🟢🔵			🟡🟢	🟡🟢🔵	🟡🟢🔵	🟡🟢🔵						
Astilbe	🟢🔵			🟢🔵	🔵	🔵	🔵						
Balloon flower	🟢🔵				🟢🔵	🟢🔵	🟢🔵						
Beard tongue	🟢🔵			🟢🔵	🟢🔵	🟢🔵	🟢🔵	🟢🔵					
Begonia	🟡🟢	🟡🟢	🟡🟢	🟡🟢	🟡🟢	🟡🟢	🟡🟢						
Bergamot	🟢🔵				🟢🔵	🟢🔵	🟢🔵						
Bergenia	🟢🔵	🟢🔵											🟢🔵
Bishop's hat	🔵	🔵	🔵	🔵									
Bleeding heart	🔵		🔵	🔵									
Campion	🟢🔵			🟢🔵	🔵	🔵	🔵						
Candelabra primula	🔵	🔵	🔵	🔵	🔵								
Canna	🟡🟢			🟡🟢	🟡🟢	🟡🟢	🟡🟢	🟡🟢					
Cardoon	🟢🔵			🟢	🟢🔵	🟢🔵	🟢🔵						
Carnation	🟢🔵	🟢	🟢🔵	🟢🔵	🔵			🟢🔵	🟢🔵	🟢🔵			
Chrysanthemum	🟢🔵								🟢🔵	🟢🔵			
Cinquefoil	🟢🔵			🟢	🟢🔵	🟢🔵	🟢🔵						
Columbine	🟢🔵		🟢🔵	🟢🔵	🔵	🔵	🔵						
Coral bells	🟢🔵	🟢🔵	🟢🔵	🟢🔵	🔵								
Coreopsis	🟢🔵		🟢	🟢	🟢🔵	🟢🔵	🟢🔵	🔵	🔵	🔵			
Corydalis	🟢🔵	🟢🔵	🟢🔵	🟢🔵	🔵	🔵	🔵						
Cranesbill	🟢🔵	🟢🔵	🟢🔵	🟢🔵	🔵	🔵	🔵						
Daylily	🟢🔵		🟢🔵	🟢🔵	🟢🔵	🟢🔵	🟢🔵	🟢🔵					
Delphinium	🟢🔵		🟢	🟢	🟢🔵	🟢🔵	🔵						
Dichorisandra	🟡🟢				🟡	🟡🟢	🟡🟢	🟡🟢					
Dietes	🟢🔵			🟢	🟢🔵	🟢🔵	🟢🔵						
Easter daisy	🟢🔵						🟢🔵	🟢🔵	🟢🔵				
Gaura	🟢🔵	🟢	🟢	🟢🔵	🟢🔵	🟢🔵	🟢🔵	🟢🔵					
Gazania	🟢🔵	🟢🔵	🟢🔵	🟢🔵	🟢🔵	🟢🔵	🟢🔵						
Geranium	🟡🟢🔵	🟡🟢	🟡🟢	🟡🟢🔵	🟡🟢🔵	🔵	🔵						
Gerbera	🟡🟢		🟡	🟡🟢	🟡🟢	🟡🟢	🟡🟢	🟡🟢	🟡🟢				
Geum	🟢🔵			🟢🔵	🟢🔵	🟢🔵	🔵						
Globe thistle	🟢🔵				🟢🔵	🟢🔵	🟢🔵	🔵					
Golden tuft	🟢🔵		🟢🔵	🟢🔵									
Gunnera	🟢🔵				🟢🔵								
Gymea lily	🟢	🟢	🟢	🟢	🟢	🟢	🟢						
Honey flower	🟡🟢				🟡🟢	🟡🟢	🟡🟢						
Hosta	🟢🔵			🟢🔵	🟢🔵	🟢🔵	🔵						
Hot water plant	🟡🟢				🟡🟢	🟡🟢	🟡🟢	🟡🟢					
Jacob's ladder	🟢🔵			🟢🔵	🔵	🔵	🔵						
Japanese windflower	🟢🔵						🟢	🟢🔵	🟢🔵				

CLIMATE KEY — TROPICAL — WARM — COOL

PLANT COMMON NAME	SUITABLE CLIMATE	SPRING EARLY	SPRING MID	SPRING LATE	SUMMER EARLY	SUMMER MID	SUMMER LATE	AUTUMN EARLY	AUTUMN MID	AUTUMN LATE	WINTER EARLY	WINTER MID	WINTER LATE
Kangaroo paw	Warm, Cool	Warm	Warm	Warm, Cool	Warm, Cool	Warm, Cool							
Kingfisher daisy	Warm, Cool	Warm, Cool	Warm, Cool	Warm, Cool	Warm, Cool	Warm, Cool	Warm, Cool	Warm	Warm	Warm			
Lady's mantle	Warm, Cool			Warm, Cool	Cool	Cool							
Lamb's ears	Warm, Cool				Warm, Cool	Warm, Cool	Cool						
Lewisia	Cool			Cool	Cool	Cool							
Liriope	Warm, Cool						Warm, Cool	Warm, Cool					
Lobelia	Warm, Cool				Warm, Cool	Warm, Cool	Warm, Cool						
Lungwort	Cool	Cool	Cool	Cool									
Lupin	Cool			Cool	Cool								
Marguerite daisy	Tropical, Warm, Cool	Tropical, Warm	Tropical, Warm	Tropical, Warm, Cool	Tropical, Warm, Cool	Cool	Cool						
Matilija poppy	Warm, Cool		Warm, Cool	Warm, Cool	Cool	Cool	Cool						
Meadow rue	Warm, Cool			Warm, Cool	Cool	Cool	Cool						
Meconopsis	Cool			Cool	Cool	Cool	Cool						
Milfoil	Warm, Cool				Warm, Cool	Warm, Cool	Warm, Cool	Warm, Cool					
Miscanthus	Warm, Cool						Warm, Cool	Warm, Cool					
Mullein	Warm, Cool	Warm, Cool	Warm, Cool	Warm, Cool	Warm, Cool	Cool							
Obedient plant	Warm, Cool					Warm, Cool	Warm, Cool	Warm, Cool					
Oyster plant	Tropical, Warm, Cool			Tropical, Warm	Cool	Cool							
Pasque flower	Cool	Cool	Cool	Cool									
Patersonia	Warm, Cool	Warm	Warm, Cool	Warm, Cool	Warm, Cool	Warm, Cool							
Pelargonium	Warm, Cool		Warm	Warm, Cool	Warm, Cool	Warm, Cool	Cool						
Peony	Cool		Cool	Cool	Cool								
Perennial phlox	Warm, Cool				Warm, Cool	Warm, Cool	Warm, Cool	Cool					
Peruvian lily	Warm, Cool		Warm, Cool	Warm, Cool	Warm, Cool	Warm, Cool	Warm, Cool	Warm, Cool					
Pinks	Warm, Cool	Warm, Cool	Warm, Cool	Warm, Cool	Warm, Cool	Warm, Cool	Warm, Cool	Cool					
Primrose	Warm, Cool	Warm, Cool	Warm, Cool	Cool									Warm
Purple coneflower	Warm, Cool						Warm, Cool	Warm, Cool	Cool				
Red hot poker	Warm, Cool			Warm, Cool	Warm, Cool	Warm, Cool	Warm, Cool	Warm, Cool					
Red valerian	Warm, Cool	Warm	Warm, Cool	Warm, Cool	Warm, Cool	Warm, Cool	Warm, Cool	Cool					
Rock rose	Cool		Cool	Cool	Cool	Cool							
Salvia	Warm, Cool				Warm, Cool	Warm, Cool	Warm, Cool	Warm, Cool	Warm, Cool	Warm, Cool			
Sea lavender	Warm, Cool		Warm	Warm	Warm, Cool	Warm, Cool	Warm, Cool	Cool					
Shasta daisy	Warm, Cool			Warm, Cool	Warm, Cool	Warm, Cool	Warm, Cool						
Sneezeweed	Warm, Cool						Warm, Cool	Warm, Cool	Warm, Cool				
Solomon's seal	Cool	Cool	Cool	Cool									
Spiderwort	Warm, Cool		Warm, Cool	Warm, Cool	Warm, Cool	Warm, Cool	Warm, Cool						
Stokes' aster	Warm, Cool				Warm, Cool	Warm, Cool	Warm, Cool	Warm, Cool					
Stone crop	Warm, Cool			Warm	Warm	Warm, Cool	Cool	Cool					
Swamp rose mallow	Warm, Cool					Warm, Cool	Warm, Cool	Warm, Cool					
Thrift	Warm, Cool	Warm, Cool	Warm, Cool	Warm, Cool	Cool	Cool							
Violet	Warm, Cool	Warm, Cool	Warm, Cool	Warm, Cool									Warm, Cool
Winter rose	Warm, Cool	Warm, Cool										Warm, Cool	Warm, Cool

INDEX

Published by Murdoch Books®, a division of Murdoch Magazines Pty Ltd,
213 Miller Street, North Sydney NSW 2060

Managing Editor, Craft & Gardening: Christine Eslick
Designer: Jackie Richards
Photographs: Lorna Rose (all unless specified otherwise); Margaret Hanks (85L); Murdoch Books® Picture Library (32L, 57L, 59 top R, 106L)
Illustrations: Sonya Naumov

CEO & Publisher: Anne Wilson
International Sales Director: Mark Newman

National Library of Australia
Cataloguing-in-Publication Data
Hanks, Margaret
A grower's guide to perennials
Includes index. ISBN 0 86411 594 6. 1. Perennials. 2. Flower gardening. I. Title. 635.932

Printed by Prestige Litho, Queensland

Acknowledgements
The publisher thanks the following for allowing photography in their gardens: Mrs Dell Adam, Cheltenham NSW (12 bottom); Mr & Mrs Anderson, Wahroonga NSW (69L & R, 87L); J. & P. Andren, Molong NSW (73L & R); Ashcombe Maze, Shoreham Vic. (97R); Sharon Beverley-Schack, Killara NSW (62R); Gordon Boots, Canberra ACT (85 bottom R, 86L & R); Bringalbit, Sidonia Vic. (28R); Don Burke's garden, Southern Highlands NSW (96L); Buskers End, Bowral NSW (inside front cover, 9, 15, 22R, 26R, 36R, 65, 71R, 107R); Mr & Mrs Byrnes, Turramurra NSW (23R); Calthorpes House, Canberra ACT (64L); Mr & Mrs Andrew Cannon, Manildra NSW (78L); Cherry Cottage, Mt Wilson NSW (34R); Colorwise Nursery, Glenorie NSW (13, 72R); Convent Gallery, Daylesford Vic. (64R); Cooramilla Nursery, Browns Creek NSW (20L, 52R, 53R, 76R, 88, 101L); E. Cossil & T. Carlstrom, Frenchs Forest NSW (14); Dr G. Cummins, Pymble NSW (52L, 54R); Mr & Mrs Davey, Castlemaine Vic. (37); Dunedin, St Leonards Tas. (31R); Forget-Me-Not Nursery, Daylesford Vic. (75L); Foxglove Spires, Tilba Tilba NSW (66R); Galapagos Farm, Bruny Island Tas. (105L); Mary Glasson, Molong NSW (40R); Gowan Brae, Burradoo NSW (10, 22L, 28L, 35L & R, 92L); Mrs Bette Hardwicke, Pymble NSW (63L); Heronswood, Dromana Vic. (17, 80L & R); Hibiscus Park Nursery, Warriewood NSW (104L, C & R); Hillview, Exeter NSW (67R, 70L); Kennerton Green, Mittagong NSW (78R, 90); Kiah Park, Jaspers Brush NSW (4, 51R, 89R); Pat & Selwyn Lawrence, Hunterville NZ (12 top, 105R); Lawrence's Nursery, Mirboo North Vic. (31L, 42L); Betty Maloney, Frenchs Forest NSW (56R); Mercure Hotel, Heritage Park, Bowral NSW (27L, 57R); Ros Mitchell, Canberra ACT (29L, 39L, 40L, 74L, 81R); Moidart, Bowral NSW (43R); Mt Tomah Botanic Gardens, NSW (43L, 47R, 59L, 92R); Pinehills, Bathurst NSW (107L); Plassy, Pipers Creek Vic. (39R, 67L, 71L, 81L); Jenny & Shane Porteus, Medlow Bath NSW (24R); Red Cow Farm, Sutton Forest NSW (7 top, 20R, 53L); Mrs Riek, Canberra ACT (85 top right); Royal Botanic Gardens, Sydney NSW (30R, 41L, 44L & R, 48L & R, 77L & R, 79L & R, 89L, 91L & R); Dora Scott, Wahroonga NSW (5, 19L, 21L & R, 24L, 38R, 41R, 42R, 74R, 87R, 98L, 102R); Mrs Smith, Orange NSW (46R, 54L, 61L & R, 70R); Swane's Nursery, Dural NSW (63R); Mrs Pat Taylor, Pymble NSW (18L, 72L); Judy & John Thompson, Canberra ACT (36L); Titoki Point, Taihape NZ (16, 29R, 55L & R, 58, 59 bottom R, 75R); Audrey & Rodney Tonkin, Orange NSW (26L, 27R, 101R); Tregamere, Te Awamutu NZ (7 bottom); Susan & John Wallace, Taumarunui NZ (100R); Sylvia Watson, Mosman NSW (66L); Welby Garden Centre, Southern Highlands Challenge Foundation, Welby NSW (94R); Sandra Wilson, Epping NSW (6, 8). A number of the gardens listed above are open under Australia's Open Garden Scheme

Front cover: Red lupins
Back cover: Top left: daylily; top centre: bishop's hat; top right: pasque flower. Bottom left: dichorisandra; bottom centre: gaura; bottom right: swamp rose mallow
Inside front cover: Milfoil (*Achillea taygetea*) and purple salvia (*Salvia sclarea*)
Title page: Winter rose (*Helleborus foetidus*)

DRAWN BY FRIENDSHIP

The art and wit of

The Revd. John Thomas Wilson

Compiled by

ANNE R. BRADFORD

First published in Great Britain by Anne R. Bradford
49, Lyonsdown Avenue, New Barnet, Herts EN5 1DX

British Library Cataloguing-in-Publication Data: a catalogue record for this book is available from the British Library.

ISBN NO. O 95O5 968 2 5

Printed in England by Redwood Books, Trowbridge, Wilts